PRAYING WITH
AND FOR OTHERS

PRAYING WITH
AND FOR OTHERS

William J. Byron, SJ

Paulist Press
New York/Mahwah, NJ

Cover design by Sharyn Banks
Book design by Lynn Else

Library of Congress Cataloging-in-Publication Data

Byron, William J., 1927–
  Praying with and for others / William J. Byron.
    p. cm.
  ISBN 978-0-8091-4518-8 (alk. paper)
  1. Prayer—Christianity. 2. Intercessory prayer. I. Title.
  BV210.3.B98 2008
  248.3'2—dc22

2007030215

Published by Paulist Press
997 Macarthur Boulevard
Mahwah, New Jersey 07430

www.paulistpress.com

Printed and bound in the
United States of America

Contents

❧ ❧

Dedication to the memory of
Elinor M. Langton, M.D., my Aunt Else,
a woman of faith and psychiatrist of note

Introduction

✒ ❧

This book is a sequel to *A Book of Quiet Prayer* (Paulist, 2006) where, in the Introduction, I made a few points that need to be repeated here:

> The entire Christian world knows that when Jesus taught his followers how to pray, he did not tell them to say, "My Father." Rather, he instructed them to say, "Our Father," and gave them the other famous words that make up what is known worldwide as "The Lord's Prayer." I want to make the point here at the outset that a book like this can, if the reader/user is not careful, encourage a person to come to prayer with a preoccupation on the "my," the self, and a forgetfulness of the "our" dimension of the approach to God.
>
> "I" have troubles and needs that drive me to pray, but so do "we"—worldwide troubles and needs. To try to go to God without any concern for the needs, joys, fears, hopes, and happiness of others, is to display a solipsistic self-centeredness that is unworthy of both the one who prays and the God to whom one lifts his or her mind and heart in prayer. Nothing at all wrong with praying alone, in private and solitude; the mistake is to

think you can or should detach yourself from the rest of the human race in order to be in solitude and alone in prayer. Before God, each one of us is all of us.

That book ended with a promise—at least to myself—that there would be a sequel that would help the one who prays to bring his or her concerns *for others* before God where, indeed, "each one of us is all of us." We cannot go to God alone. Nor should we forget, when facing God, that there are persons and problems out there in need of our prayers, and that praying with, not simply for, but *with* others, extends our reach and raises our silent or vocal prayers to higher levels of effectiveness. Hence this book about prayer "with and for others."

You, my reader friend, have, I know, a lot on your mind. In fact, you often complain that you cannot pray your way through the multiple distractions that race through your mind. Some of you put it honestly, although inaccurately, this way: "I can't sit still long enough to pray. I'm always distracted. I just can't pray."

You are not speaking falsely when you say that, because that is what you are convinced is true. But it is inaccurate. Your problem is not unlike the difficulty encountered by professional "pray-ers," those men and women who enter monastic or religious life and "profess" the vows of religion and try to measure up to the ideal, spelled out in St. Paul's command to "pray without ceasing" (1 Thess 5:17) or, as Jesus put it in an instruction to his apostles, "pray always without losing heart."

St. Augustine, in a "Discourse on the Psalms (Psalm 17)," offered wise advice when he interpreted Paul's words this way:

> Are we then ceaselessly to bend our knees, to lie prostrate, or to lift up our hands? Is this what is meant in saying *Pray without ceasing*? Even if we admit that we pray in this fashion, I do not believe that we can do so all the time. Yet there is another, interior kind of prayer without ceasing, namely, the desire of the heart…if you wish to pray without ceasing, do not cease to desire.

The comparison I'm trying to forge here is simply this. Let the problems that distract you, your concerns about the needs and welfare of others, your preoccupation with the problems of the world, let all that "stuff" on your mind that prevents you, you say, from praying, become the "stuff" of your prayer. Just as your deep-down desire for God is always there and amounts, Augustine says, to your "prayer without ceasing," so your distractions and worldly preoccupations are, in fact, prayers from you to God. In working your way through them, you are working your way toward God.

This small book is offered as a help along the way. And what I attempt here is, I believe, consistent with a view expressed centuries ago by the great St. John Chrysostom, who, after referring to prayer as "a partnership and union with God," said: "I do not mean the prayer of outward observance but prayer from the heart, not confined to fixed times or periods but continuous throughout the day and night. Our spirit should be quick to reach out toward God, not only when it is engaged in meditation; at other times also, when it is carrying out its duties, caring for the needy, performing works of charity, giving generously in the service of others, our spirit should long for God and call him to mind, so that these works may be seasoned with the salt of God's love."

Praying "with and for" others adds salt and balance to your partnership with God.

Loyola College in Maryland
Thanksgiving Day 2006

PART ONE
Praying for Others

When Jesus specified that we pray not to "My Father," but to "Our Father," he may well have been making the point that your heart has to be open to others when you approach the Lord in prayer. Praying with others, in community with others, is a preferred approach to God who made his covenant with us as a people, not as isolated individuals. This is not to say that praying alone is inappropriate or ineffective; it is just not *as* effective as praying with, in, and from the community of the faithful.

Think how that word "for" finds its way around in ordinary usage. McCarthy comes in "for" (in place of) Johnson to pitch in the top of the ninth. I'm headed "for" (toward) Boston after stopping off in New York. I'd do anything "for" (to assist) my friend, who, by the way, will be my friend "for" (the duration of) life. I'd give anything "for" (to have) a cold beer. I'm "for" (on the side of) the Cubs in good seasons and bad. Put in a good word "for" me (on my behalf). I'm "for" you (meaning with you) all the way.

And so it goes in praying for another. You can pray for another by praying in his or her place. I admired a father's love that prompted him to stand in and participate, as if he were ill, in a communal healing service, "for" his daughter who was ill and could not be present in church for the service. I admired another father's love when he gave up drinking alcoholic beverages for a year as a petition to God "for" (an exchange) his daughter's recovery to health. Praying "for" peace requires the staying power of a committed person who knows that peace will not come suddenly, but that prayers for peace can move us in the right direction.

Praying "for" another can be much like putting in a good word "for" (on behalf of) a friend in need. You can pray for another simply because that other person asked you to. You can pray for someone you don't know; you only know him or her to be in need. You can pray for someone you know very well, but who perhaps might be a stranger to prayer and feels no need for God's help. Mothers and fathers find themselves doing this all the time. You can pray for persons completely unknown to you, for persons not yet born. You can and should pray for those who have died.

Upon receiving word recently that a friend had died, I found myself saying, "May God be good to him." And I then stopped to ask how God could be anything but good to him and to all of us who are God's very own. We are foolish enough at times to be bad to ourselves by fending off God's goodness, by refusing to permit God to be good to us. God, for his part, can be nothing but good all the time. In praying for others, we are always praying that they will be open to the reception of what the all-good God knows to be best for them. So here begins, my reader friend, a reflection and roundup of prayer for others. You may have your own prayer list, a ballot of those for whom you cast your prayer-vote often, if not every day. Make room on that list for me, as I make room here for you to route yourself randomly in and through the prayer-for-others categories that make up Part One of this book.

1. Family

Tolstoy's novel *Anna Karenina* has this famous opening sentence: "All happy families are alike, but an unhappy family is unhappy after its own fashion."

You have to wonder how any family anywhere could come into being without a prayer. Sadly, I know, some marriages begin without much thought to prayer and no formal prayer at all in what passes for a wedding ceremony. But even from that unpromising beginning, prayer of some sort is more than likely to surround the "blessed event" of childbirth and accompany the hesitant steps of first parenthood. As the family grows, it is more than likely that some form of prayer will find its way into family life, and most regrettable if it does not.

You also have to ask yourself about the power of prayer in healing unhappy families, or in helping other families hold onto happiness before it slips away. Plenty of books are available to help unhappy family members puzzle out what may have gone wrong and what might be done to bring things back into some kind of balance; this is not one of them. This book is a resting place, a port in a storm, a roadmap for the searching heart, a companion in moments of solitude. Some of those moments will be spent with family in mind.

If you want to pray for a better world, pray that families will become stronger. Strengthening families means strengthening the bonds of love between husband and wife, and the parents' love for those whose lives are the fruit of spousal love. Praying for families in general is to pray for a strengthening of the social fabric. Praying for a particular family is to wish that family well, and to ask God, who is the source of everything that is good, to fill that family with goodness, to be very good to them.

Sometimes praying "for a family" means praying for fertility, for the ability to conceive and bring a child to birth. That amounts to asking to be brought into partnership with God, the author of life. An awareness of God's presence accompanies the sense of wonder associated with holding a newborn child and realizing that nothing in your hands was made by human hands. In wonder, then, let yourself pray.

⌁

For families, Lord, I want to pray.

For families past, I pray a word of gratitude.

For families present, I beg your protection,
your guidance, your forgiveness.

Without family, human persons literally cannot
know who they are,

and cannot even begin to grasp who you are either.

You are family to me, good Lord, there for me always,
ready to take me in.

You nurture me—like family.

You forgive me more readily than my own family
forgiveness could touch me.

Let me be forgiveness to others in my family.

You protect me not as if I were,
but because I am, your own.

That's family.

And that's why I turn to you in prayer for families,
for all families everywhere,

for any family in need.

Some of the neediest families I know are not
economically poor, Lord;

they are well off in worldly goods, but badly
off course in the quest for happiness.

I guess it is true that every unhappy family has its
own unique way of being unhappy.

But it is also true that you have your own unique
way of straightening things out.

So please, Lord, just because I'm asking you,
straighten out and strengthen our families

and support them in service of life.

❦

2. Friends

Praying "for friends" could mean a prayer to find a friend, to have good friends whom you can count on, faithful friends with whom you can share life's journey. Praying to have friends is a form of wise provisioning because you won't get far in life without them. Take a moment every now and then to pray, if you will, for protection against friend-lessness. It is prayer time well spent.

Because they are so essential for your own well-being, pray in thanksgiving for the friends you have. Show your love for your friends by commending them to God who, of course, knows and loves them more than you ever could, but, because this is God's way of doing things, wants to be reminded by you that your friends have needs. Show your concern for them by praying that their needs will be met. Pray that nothing but good will come to them. And, when hardship befalls them, when reversals come their way, pray that they will have the strength to bear their burdens; pray that they will have the vision to see through their troubles to the loving God who is always faithful, always standing by, and who never stops reaching out to them.

Anything that's ever been said about a port in a storm, or a life raft, or a safety net, can be said about a good friend. Your friends, like you, stand in need at times of the kind of port, raft, and net that you and your prayers can provide. You may, in fact, become for them what is so often called the "answer to a prayer"—their prayer, not yours, although at other times they may emerge as the answer to your own prayers in time of need.

This mutuality and reciprocity are caught in an old Latin expression that has for centuries been part of the monastic tradition, *oremus pro invicem*. Let's pray for one another. That's a pact worth making with any friend. It is a pact that will strengthen the bond of friendship.

"Friends don't let friends drive drunk," say the public service radio announcements. You've long been aware that "a friend in need is a friend indeed." You also know that "friendship needs no words" and that "who finds a faithful friend finds a treasure." In prayer you can thank God for the treasure of friendship. You can be silent before God just thinking of your friend. You should be alert to your friend's needs. And from your prayer you can draw the necessary strength to speak the truth with love to a friend, and, when necessary, protect a friend from his or her excesses.

The seasons come and go; strong friendships can endure.

⌒

Let me pause to thank you once again,
Lord, for the gift of friendship.

And as I do, let me beg forgiveness
for my failures as a friend.

I'm both fragile and fickle, needing friends
more than they need me.

But, wonder of wonders, I am able
to be a friend to others.

Shore me up in my friendship commitments.

Help me to be loyal.

Remind me to listen.

Enable me to reach out.

*And since your way of doing things, Lord,
is to have us gain by giving,*

let me enjoy true friendship, to have it and to hold it;

*and to realize that friendship comes not to those
who wait, but to those who give,*

and give, and give again.

⟋⟍

3. Associates

Not long after "personnel directors" gave way to "human resource managers" in the world of work, the "employees" who once populated the workplace became "associates." It used to amuse me to hear executives refer to persons they hardly knew, and with whom they rarely if ever socialized, as "associates." But now it is common to speak of associates rather than employees, and the change in nomenclature is not at all a bad idea.

A Latin word for friend is *socius*. Your *socius* is your ally, your companion, your friend. "Associations" bring people of like mind together for some common purpose. You choose not to "associate" with those whom you do not trust and whose values you do not share. Some of your associations are close and personal; others may be remote.

Not to be lost is the social dimension of association in any context; the friendship side of the presence of associates in the workplace is a special gift. Just as you cannot be expected to like everyone you meet (you are only required to love them!), you are not likely to become great friends with all whom you encounter on the job. Nonetheless, it is both healthy (for you) and generous (toward them) to be mindful of your associates when you take time out to pray.

I was touched years ago to hear of a teacher who often took her class list with her into the chapel for a period of prayer. Commend them to the Lord, your associates; ask God to bless them, encourage them, ease their anxieties, sustain their efforts. When you pray for those with whom you share any space at all in the world of work, you are also praying for yourself. Your progress is a function of theirs since the entire organization moves forward together. Your productivity is enhanced by theirs, regardless of who gets the credit.

A significant portion of your life is spent with those whom you meet at life's great workbench. It is surely myopic for a believer not to imagine having a place with them at the banquet table in God's kingdom. So pray for them now even though workplace conventions rarely if ever set the stage for formal prayer. Just commend them to the Lord as quietly and naturally as you take in and breathe out your workplace air. And be sure to think of them, your associates, when you have a few quiet moments with the Lord away from the busyness of work. Then you might find yourself praying in words like these.

*It is more than blind chance or fate
that brings me together with others in*

the workplace, Lord.

*I know that because the skills and talents
that make us suitable for employment*

*are your gifts to us; you give according to plan,
not randomly.*

So I thank you, Lord, for placing them next to me,

and putting me in companionship with them.

*Together we can fulfill your will, praise you, and find
meaning in our separate selves.*

I pray especially, Lord, for those I don't much like,

*and can't help but notice that what
I don't much like in them*

is also part of me.

*May that recognition be the beginning
of wisdom for me, Lord.*

I'll never fully understand my associates, I know;

I'll never be able to read their hearts or feel their pain.

So let me not be judgmental, Lord.

*Remind me from time to time that I have a lot
to be humble about,*

*and that a kind word of gratitude or
encouragement could be the toll*

you want me to pay in crossing the bridges
you build between me and

my associates. Amen.

∼∼

4. Enemies

One of seven inscriptions carved on the walls at the gravesite of President John F. Kennedy mentions enemies—not personal but "common enemies"—that should be kept in mind when you turn to prayer. In his January 20, 1961, inaugural address, President Kennedy said: "Now the trumpet summons us again—not as a call to bear arms, though arms we need; not as a call to battle, though embattled we are—but a call to bear the burden of a long twilight struggle, year in and year out, 'rejoicing in hope, patient in tribulation'—a struggle against the common enemies of man: tyranny, poverty, disease and war itself." These are surely things to pray about. The list can easily be lengthened. Hunger is an enemy. So is cancer. Hostile forces like these array themselves against you and your brothers and sisters in the worldwide human community.

The "enemies within" provide material for prayer. Personal weaknesses, addictions, pride, and all other "disordered affections," as the spiritual writers would label them. You are the world's leading expert on your personal inventory of these disorders. One way of beginning to root them out is to lay them out before God in prayer.

More commonly, we think of enemies as those who treat us badly, those by whom we have been "done in" in one way or another. Just thinking of them and the harm they have done raises up for your consideration the question of forgiveness. You have to be ready to forgive when you bring your personal enemies to prayer. Even if harm has not yet come your way, the one who threatens to harm you looms large as an enemy. Any enemy, actual or potential, is one you have to be prepared to love.

Love your enemies; do good to those who hate you. This is what the Gospel requires of the Christian faithful. Other faith traditions impose various obligations of regard for enemies. All faith traditions, and human reason itself, recognize the destructive potential of hatred. Enemies must be dealt with constructively, not destroyed. Enmity can be dissolved when that which is most human within us is permitted to surface and take control. The command to love your enemies is a call to do what your deepest human longing, your truest self, wants to do. You therefore have to avoid painting yourself into a vindictive corner where striking back is your only apparent alternative. You can do much better. And you will do better if you wrap yourself in preventive prayer "against" your enemies.

⌒

Lord, I pray for those who have done me wrong,
and I pray for those who appear prepared to do me in.
I need your help in bringing myself to forgive them.
I know real harm when it comes my way;
I've had what I consider to be more than my share.

But I'm frightened by my tendency to imagine harm,
with no known source,

coming at me.

A little bit of "thinking defensively"
is only prudent, I know;

but I tend to want to arm myself against all sorts
of enemies, real and imagined,

so I need your help in thinking positively
and living peacefully.

Help me to make friends of my enemies.

Prevent me from letting myself become an enemy to others.

With fewer enemies and more friends, the world cannot
be anything but a better place.

And that's the kind of place I'm searching for.

5. Strangers

"I was a stranger, and you took me in" is a familiar scriptural quotation. Irreverent wags sometimes use "you took me in" in the sense of bait and switch, fraud, or deceit, and prompt a bit of laughter by implying that the "righteous" do not always deal with strangers in the way this text presumes.

It is our fate in modern times to be surrounded by strangers, even in settings that are intended for community and friendship. Those who worship in large congregations, typically worship amidst strangers. Those who travel in buses, trains, and planes find themselves in the midst of strangers. Employment in large organizations means identifying one-self organizationally more with strangers than with friends.

Children are taught not to talk to strangers and warned never to walk off with a stranger. For children, a stranger is anyone they do not know. Understandably, this leads to fear of strangers. Think of the millions who would quite properly regard you as a stranger and you can smile when you ask yourself what would anyone have to fear from you.

From your perspective, the stranger is associated with the unknown and unfamiliar, but from the stranger's point of view, what strikes you as strange, is completely known and totally familiar. It all depends on your point of view.

It is broadening, to say the least, to educate oneself in the ways of others, their history, language, preferences, habits, customs. That's why it is so often said that travel is broaden-ing. There are many ways to travel without leaving home. Books, magazines, and the *Discovery Channel*, along with conversations with persons whose background is not your own, are opportunities to broaden your outlook. But no mat-ter how extensive your outreach in this regard, the unknowns will remain and the strangers will dominate your universe.

If you can let yourself begin to appreciate the dominant ratio of strangers-to-you in the world you share with them, you gain a glimpse of the range of God's perspective on a world filled, not with strangers, but with unique persons cre-ated and known by God. You take a God-like view when you look out in prayer on a world filled with human beings who are strangers to you but "well knowns" to God.

From that perspective, let yourself pray:

*It is your world, Lord, that I'm seeing now
with my mind's eye.*

*It is a world filled with persons who are known
and loved by you, but strangers to me.*

*I can only imagine the extent of the pain
that others in this world suffer,*

*the hunger that so many endure, the hatred
that assails them, the disease that*

*robs them of life, the countless assaults
on their human dignity.*

Can't you help them, Lord?

Yes, I know you can.

Why won't you help them, Lord?

*I guess I know the answer to that question too.
It lies somewhere in your plan of*

helping those whom you've created

by having them love and help one another.

I'm sure not doing my part.

But even so, how can you stand by and not do anything?

*I hear you turning that question around and
pointing it back to me, Lord:*

How can I stand by and do nothing?

Nudge me, please, toward helping strangers,
especially the poor and needy.

Take away my fears.

Help me trim back my selfishness.

Inspire me to share with strangers.

And promise me that in some stranger, somewhere,
I'll catch a glimpse of you.

6. Workers

If you are one who has others working for you, "reporting to you," as they say in the corporate world, ask yourself if you ever pray for them—for their health, happiness, and eternal salvation. If that notion strikes you as quaint, or makes you feel uncomfortable, take it as a measure of the gap between matter and spirit in your life. The spiritual should indeed matter to you and hold a high place on your value scale. But it won't count for much if you make no room for the spiritual in practical matters. And where are matters more practical than in the world of work?

Workers deserve your prayers. Where would you be without the work of others? Simple justice calls for a prayer of gratitude for those whose labor, applied intelligence, competence, and directed energy enliven the world of work. From their efforts emerge what you need to sustain and enjoy life.

Workers young and old, black and white, organized and unorganized, skilled and unskilled, employed and unemployed, deserve a place on your prayer card. The world of work, as a subset of "the world" considered in global terms, is a worthy subject of meditative reflection. Work is, after all, God's gift to us, a means by which we realize our potential and give our talents a good stretch. Work is the way we serve one another (and thus show our love for one another). For most of us, work functions as a range-finder in our search for meaning in life. Those who fall behind or are left out of the world of work stand in need of prayer in their struggle to get back on track.

There is more to life than work, of course. And there is more to any worker than a function performed. We are, after all, human beings not human doings, and we have to guard against defining ourselves or anyone else in terms of what we do. We especially have to guard against the great American secular heresy that what you do is what you are, and when you "do nothing" (are unemployed or in retirement), you *are* nothing. So much self-esteem has been crushed under the weight of that false conclusion! And there is so much arrogance displayed by those who view low-skill or menial work as unimportant and those who perform it as "nothings."

I know of a business school professor who puts the following question, worth 15 points, on his mid-term examination: "What is the name of the worker who cleans this classroom and the corridor outside?" His response to the howls of protest from angry students: "I'm just preparing you to become a good employer. If you don't know the little people by name, you won't be providing good leadership in your organization. And if you think the question was unfair,

I'll make it up to you by telling you now that the same question will be on the final!"

No one but you is giving the tests as you work your way through these pages. I'm just inviting you now to pause and think about the work you do and to be grateful for the health, talent, education, and energy that enable you to do it. I would encourage you to think about the workers who stand behind so many of the goods and services that you tend to take for granted. Pray for them. And let me urge you to think of those who are out of work as well as those on the margins of the workforce in low-skilled, low-paying employment. Here let your view extend well beyond our borders to those who are trapped between misery and workplace exploitation. And as you pray, open up the question of what you might do to make things better in the world of work.

Thank you, Lord, for work and workers.

As creator you have given us the wherewithal to provide, through work,

for ourselves and one another;

I tend to overlook the others when I think about work.

I tend to focus too narrowly on my slice of the "wherewithal."

There are so many humans being ground under at this moment in the world of work.

Many of them, I'm told, are just kids.

*Open my eyes, open all our eyes and our hearts
as well, to them, Lord.*

*Bless us, Lord, with work for all, and with justice
in the workplace.*

*Work is your gift to us, if only we are wise enough
to see it that way.*

*I benefit from the gift of work that countless
unknown others bring to the workplace,*

and for that I'm grateful.

*I contribute my small share from my place
at the worldwide workbench,*

where I am more than grateful to have a place.

*Fire me up with enthusiasm, Lord, to make
that workbench large enough for all*

who want to work and who need to work.

*And may what we do at the workbench be our way
of serving you and one another.*

7. Students

Those who teach them should certainly pray for them. Otherwise, teachers will give students reason to believe that they, as their students sometimes suspect, like to "play God," pretending to be all-knowing and all-powerful. Teachers, of course, will always say that just isn't so. The satisfaction that teachers experience when a pedagogical spark ignites to produce a moment of understanding in a young mind is a spiritual experience. Those who reflect on that experience will gain a sense of co-creation, a feeling of working in partnership with the creator of all minds and all good things. It is a very short trip from that realization on the part of a teacher to a moment of prayer by the teacher for the student.

All of us should pray for students (and for teachers and others who provide the learning environment). It is so critically important for human happiness as well as human progress that things go well in the student years. Time lost then is lost forever. Opportunities missed might possibly return, but if the years slip by and the foundation has not fallen into place, the learning structure will not be there to support a fully productive human life.

Parents will naturally pray for their student offspring. They might find their prayers answered in terms of a previously unrecognized need for them to learn with their youngsters, to participate with them in the voyage of discovery that is not limited to classroom life. It carries over into home (homework, anyone?), to the family library of books, tapes, disks, and cyberspace connections. Parents provide the outings and the trips that have educative value in themselves. Parents, most of all, are the ones who permit their youngsters to take those risks that are indispensable to a good learning process. And parents, of course, are more likely than any others who want to help their children learn, to know that without the help of God good education just isn't going to happen.

It is interesting to note how many prayer professionals —men and women whose lives are committed to service within a given faith community—devote themselves to the education of the young. They surely pray for their charges. Their prayers are not in vain.

With all this prayer for them and around them, how might students be encouraged to pray for themselves? The "school prayer" debates in the public square always allow for individual freedom, although under the First Amendment institutional discretion may be limited in public schools with respect to public prayer. Everyone has heard the quip that so long as there are tests and exams in public schools, there will be prayer in the schools!

Regardless of where the student studies, he or she will be better served to the extent that the link between human effort and divine assistance is forged. Schools educate for life. It is better earlier than later for a student to recognize that life, though fleeting, is not a solo flight. "God is my co-pilot," said a World War II hero. Even if this truth cannot be taught in a public school classroom, it is something that can be communicated out of school by others who include all students in their prayers.

For students, Lord, let me pause to pray.
I want to begin from the top.
Graduate and professional students: Lord, encourage them.
Dissertations get delayed; lab experiments go wrong,
data disappear, and discouragement sets in.

*We need them, Lord, and we need the work
that they will do,*

*so bless them with continuing commitment
and academic success.*

*Those professional students need you more than most of
them realize, Lord,*

so I'm here to call their need to your attention.

*Shape their learning experience so that they will emerge
from their studies*

*as men and women equipped with competence, imbued
with ethics, and*

enthusiastic for human service.

*The collegiate years present you with more than
a few challenges, Lord, I know,*

but don't lose your patience with collegians.

Bring them along; protect them from their excesses.

*When they "commence" on Graduation Day,
let it be with the conviction*

*that the happy life is the life lived generously in service
to others.*

*High school years are so important, Lord. These are the
years when we worry probably*

*more than we should about students, and trust them
not enough. So let us entrust them*

now to you.

Watch over our middle schoolers, Lord;
their full potential will not be realized

if things do not go well in these tender years.
Give us wisdom to guide them

on their first steps toward wisdom.

And in the lower grades on down the
development ladder through K and pre-K,

the students there are precious treasures.

Those who teach them are privileged to
facilitate their growth.

Teachers, parents, and all the rest of us who
care about the future

commend them to you alone, Lord, who can give them
a future filled with hope.

8. Teachers

Praying for teachers is, it seems to me, a matter of simple justice. We owe them so much. And we tend to forget them too easily. If there is anything to the old joke that behind every successful man there is a surprised mother-in-law, there has to be some basis for saying that behind any successful man or woman is a little known and probably unremembered teacher.

It is a healthy exercise to let your mind run back to the year of your earliest formal education and try to recall, year by year, all the way up to the year of your last diploma or terminal degree, the names of those who taught you. Pray for them all, even those you can't remember. In acknowledging that there are some whose names and faces have slipped from memory, you have to regret your self-centeredness, indeed your selfishness, in taking what they offered, but not extending to them the courtesy of grateful remembrance.

Teachers surely aren't in it for the money. Nor are they there for praise, although a word of praise is always appreciated. Teachers are there for you when you need them in those developmental years because they have a calling. For some, I suppose, it is just a job, but they are the ones who move on to other things. Those who stay, derive deep satisfaction from participating in a process of planting, cultivating, and nurturing, a process of pruning and correcting, to be sure, but only on the way toward an eventual harvest. Teachers sow, society reaps the harvest. The student grows in a growth that produces a mature person. Any grown person who forgets, however, the teachers who cultivated their growth, still has some maturing to do.

At the Greater Washington (DC) Board of Trade's "2002 Leader of the Year" award dinner, I heard a very successful man pay a moving tribute to his third grade teacher. In his acceptance speech, John P. McDaniel, CEO of MedStar Health, told a gathering of movers and shakers in the national capital's business community, "When I was in third grade in Carey, Ohio, my teacher was Wheltha Wentling, a kindly, dedicated lady who never married and whose whole life was teaching." Why mention her on that occasion? Because, as a child, McDaniel said, he struggled with an unidentified problem that we now know as dyslexia.

"She kept me after school every afternoon," said the honoree, "working with me, teaching me how to read. I remember her saying, 'John, we're going to figure this reading thing out.' And we did."

"I didn't know it then, and wasn't even very grateful at the time," said John McDaniel, "but Wheltha Wentling changed my life. Wheltha Wentling, who reached out to a floundering young student, was a leader in the truest sense of the word."

MedStar Health is a not-for-profit health care organization integrating thirty hospitals and health care organizations in the Washington-Baltimore region. It is the fifth largest employer in the region with 22,000 on the payroll and over 4,000 affiliated physicians, serving more than half-a-million patients each year. It takes a lot of reading to be able to lead an organization like this. It took a lot of patience back in Carey, Ohio, to teach this future executive how first to read in order later to lead.

"Sister Genevieve was my sixth-grade teacher at St. Mathieu's School in Fall River, Massachusetts," said syndicated political columnist and social justice advocate E. J. Dionne, Jr., in reply to David Shribman's inquiry about most memorable teachers. "She got kicked out of the South in the 1960s because she organized a biracial communion service. She was no radical, but she taught me more than anyone else about racial justice without saying much of anything." David Shribman's book, *I Remember My Teacher,* published by Andrews McMeel, contains many more grateful tributes like this one.

Walter Sheridan's career as an investigator began after graduation from Fordham University in 1949. He went from the National Security Agency, to the FBI, on to close collaboration with Robert F. Kennedy in the 1950s on a Senate Committee investigating corruption in organized labor. When Kennedy became attorney general, Sheridan went with him to the Justice Department as a special assistant charged with the task of exposing corruption in the Teamsters Union. And when Kennedy went to the Senate, Sheridan, who once told me that the person who had the greatest influence on his life was the nun who taught him in the fifth grade in Utica, New York, became an investigative reporter for *NBC News*.

"In Defense of Honest Labor" was the way the *New York Times Magazine* summed up the career of Walter Sheridan after his death in 1995. That unnamed nun in Utica never knew that she would have anything to do with a career of a man who, as the *Times* put it, tried "to save the labor movement from the enemy within," and "help thousands of people who would never know his name." Anonymity has its own rewards!

Your teachers may be largely anonymous now, but don't forget to "say an Ave" for them from time to time, as the "Danny Boy" lyric would have you do. There is probably a surprise awaiting you on the other side of the pearly gates, where one of your forgotten teachers, who has long since disposed of chalk, pointer, and grade book, has been putting in many good words for you, cheering you on, and waiting to introduce you to all the other saints.

I'm not just forgetful, Lord; I've been ungrateful.

I've forgotten many of those who taught me,

*and I've neglected to thank you for your gift
to me in them.*

*I remember hearing a story once of a
fifth-grade teacher who left her*

*paycheck in an envelope on the desk in front of her.
When a child reached out*

*to pick it up, she said, "Careful, that's my paycheck."
And the child responded,*

"Oh, do you have a job somewhere?"

*I've been the "job," the challenge, for more than
a few teachers, Lord.*

Thank you for sending them my way.

*Thank you for gifting them with patience, which,
I suspect, seemed at times*

*more important for them than intelligence,
although intelligent they surely were.*

And generous too.

That may be what they taught us best—generosity.

*And that's why my ungenerous failure to remember them
until now embarrasses me.*

*So, I pray for my teachers, Lord, reward them
with your love.*

I also pray you to touch the hearts of some in
the ranks of today's young and generous,

so that they may see the beauty in the call to be a teacher.

Give them the grace to hear and the courage to respond.

⌁

9. Neighbors

Anyone at all familiar with the Christian Gospel is likely to think "Good Samaritan" upon hearing the word *neighbor*. Who was neighbor to the man who fell among thieves? The Samaritan, a stranger from another country, who happened to be passing by, and who had the heart to stop and help, proved himself to be a neighbor to the victim.

Presumably, a neighbor is anyone who is near. But we know that just isn't always or often the case. Without knowledge of the other, nearness to the other means little. Closeness can be the cause of discomfort or threat. Yet proximity to an unknown-other-in-need is an occasion to become a neighbor. How easy it is to let this occasion pass and to remain apart, unconnected, alone.

When Levittowns began springing up almost overnight to meet the housing shortage after World War II, observers called them "instant neighborhoods." But it takes a lot more than connecting backyards and front-door proximity to make a neighborhood. Neighborhoods are forged out of human interaction, not hammered together by carpenters and joined by masons. Engineers, architects, and builders shape physical environments; human beings shape neighbor-hood communities. Within those communities, it is relatively easy to be "neighbor" to another. But even there, we often prefer a measure of distance from the other. We prefer our own private space and want to protect our own private lives. These preferences can wrap us up in loneliness. Our choice to live apart from others can condemn us to a condition of living in need of companionship. For neighbor and neigh-borhood to come to the rescue, we have first to reach out to them, to offer a helping hand, to extend the hand of friend-ship. In doing so, we register our own call for help, and that call is answered without fanfare in the typical, normal neigh-borly response.

If there is any truth to the saying that good fences make good neighbors, and I think there is, I would suggest that personal resourcefulness makes good neighborhoods. How do you get them away from their television sets and into the book-discussion groups? How do you make pot-luck sup-pers attractive social events? How do you interest others in sharing the ride to work? Can the responsibility for child-care, lawn-care, snow removal, neighborhood security, and elder-care become a common cause with neighborhood-building potential? How can a neighborhood come up with creative leisure-time activities for the young? And so it goes. There is so much that needs doing that won't get done unless those living in proximity to one another decide to become neighbors to one another. Not to mention the challenge of building community in neighborhoods that have no lawns, no open space, just broken glass and boarded windows.

I'm involved in an effort to provide quality nondenom-
inational middle-school education for poor boys in
Washington, DC. Their economic deprivation is beyond
question. Their academic potential is strong, and each has a
mentoring adult committed to sticking with them for the
three-year journey that will prepare them for college
preparatory secondary education. In addition to intensive
work in languages and mathematics, the attention of these
boys is directed to the values needed to sustain a good and
productive life. In this context, they are invited to pray
together each day. Invariably they pray for safety in the
neighborhoods to which they will return at night. And, as
the head of the school told me, they often pray for an elderly
grandparent living in fear in a neighborhood that progress
left behind.

Any neighborhood can serve to remind one who lives
or visits there of the need to pray for those who inhabit the
houses and the hood.

⌒

You know them, Lord; they're my neighbors.

I don't always know their names,

nor do I always know their needs,

*and that is probably why I'm less than
a great neighbor to them.*

I notice that they don't always get along

and they often seem not to understand one another;

*but what do I really know about that since
I'm not close enough*

to even begin

to understand?

I admit to choosing to be too busy to be a good neighbor.

*I also admit to being in need of the human reinforcement
that good neighbors can give.*

*If I break out of my self-enclosure and extend
myself to them, Lord,*

will you prompt them to open up to me?

I'm not trying to make a deal;

*I'm just letting you know what you already know:
that I'm in need of help.*

That's what neighbors are for.

Neighbor to neighbor.

It works both ways, I know.

It won't work at all unless I make my move.

*So, I'm thinking now about "moving in" by
"moving out" toward them.*

Move me toward action, Lord.

*It might just save me from myself and help to save
a neighborhood as well.*

10. Patients

Do you remember the confusion you encountered as a child trying to keep "patients" and "patience" straight? If you were lucky enough to study Latin in high school, you ran across *passio* and were told it meant "suffering." Then more confusion closed in as you wondered what connection the English word *passion*, related obviously to *passio*, might have with the idea of suffering. The movie posters and the back covers of paperback novels used the word *passion* to suggest pleasure, not pain.

Eventually you came to understand that the agent acts and the patient receives the action. Action from without can cause suffering within. The patient is one who suffers. The person who bears up under pain, inconvenience, insult, discourtesy, and delay is thought to be patient. Pain at the hands of a physician or dentist is the fate of the patient whose supply of patience may or may not be very large. Those suffering pain typically present themselves as patients to nurses, doctors, and others skilled in the healing arts.

Regardless of your present supply of patience, pause for a moment now to think of those who might properly be called patients—those in hospital rooms, emergency rooms, operating rooms, recovery rooms. Think of those in long-term care—residents of nursing homes and assisted living centers. Out-patients, in-patients, patients being admitted, patients being discharged—all, by definition, need some help, and, whether they know it or not, they could benefit from your prayers.

Most people admit that patience is not their strong suit.
Most people find it difficult to play the patient's role
patiently. And yet they must be patient in the presence of the
healing hand that reaches out to help.

⌒

Into your hands, Lord, I commend all patients
in this world.

Short-term, long-term, acutely ill, or temporarily
out of circulation,

the patients I pray for need to be reminded that
they are chosen to be saints.

Serious sickness can, by your providence,
be a staging area for the journey

home to heaven.

Most of us are very patient about waiting to
take that trip, but not at all patient

about the timing of our return to health and home.

We want to rush back.

We want to get out, go home, return to work,
family, and friends.

We are more than willing to break all speed limits
on the road to recovery.

We don't easily see the redemptive value in suffering,

but I believe it's there.

And so I pray, Lord, that those who suffer will
see the power in their pain

*and turn that power to the benefit of others who need
God's saving grace,*

which, mysteriously, God grants to those who ask for it,

*especially those who permit their pain to give
voice to their plea.*

*I also pray for their return to health, to their families,
and to the company of their*

friends, if that might be your will for them,

*"Pain makes one think. Thought makes one wise.
And wisdom makes life endurable,"*

said an actor in a play I saw long ago.

Lord, I ask you to make me wise enough to be patient,

and patient enough to endure all things

for my own good and the good of all the world.

∼

11. Prisoners

A whole new book could begin right here, but it would not
add much to the body of prison literature because my experience with prisons and prisoners is limited. Much has been
written about prison life. Theoretical studies, historical
accounts, and moving personal stories try to address a need
for better understanding of rehabilitation and corrections.
We have to think straight about helping criminals go straight.
The reconstruction of broken lives is the challenge con-
fronting anyone who is troubled by the facts of prison life.

The statistics are grim. Evidence of genuine rehabilitation is virtually nonexistent. Recidivism rates are high. The disproportionate number of African-American and Hispanic inmates is obvious. The average levels of educational attainment are appallingly low in local, county, state, and federal prisons. Poverty has a cultural link to criminal behavior. If the culture of poverty persists, the jails will always be full. Drug-related offenses account for an alarmingly high percentage of prison populations.

Readers of this book are not likely to have much personal experience of prisons and prisoners. Some who are serving or have served time for white-collar crime may be known to you, my reader friend, and may be persons who could find both purpose and comfort in these pages. The same might be said for short-term inmates who find themselves in jail because of fractured domestic relations. Incarceration is not a pleasant experience for anyone. Everyone in jail needs the support of your prayers.

I've visited a few prisons over the years, usually to see an individual inmate; I walk away every time feeling depressed. Visitors to mental hospitals, cancer wards, tenements, and slums have reason to walk away depressed. But nothing I've encountered saddens me like the spectacle of men or women behind bars. It is difficult for them to preserve their human dignity. They have virtually no privacy. The air is heavy, odors noticeable, noise incessant, and the evident loneliness in the midst of heavy concentrations of humanity is aggravated by the absence of any words of encouragement and love. Those sentiments have to come from within the soul and spirit of the prisoner. That soul may be "on ice" and the spirit may have sunk into the depths of hopelessness. This is why prisoners, most of whom will be unknown to you, deserve a place in your prayers.

∽

Lord, if you are everywhere, as I believe you are,

I have to conclude that you are there in the prisons that are on my mind at the moment.

Imprisoned would not be the right term, I know, but in prison you are,

somehow, in some mysterious way, because you are everywhere.

One form of your presence there is by virtue of your presence within every prisoner.

Some may be inhospitable to you.

Some welcome your presence and try not to deface your image within themselves.

Some neither care about nor reverence your presence; they open their

hearts to evil and you are present to them by preserving them in existence.

If you chose to forget them, they would cease to exist.

So let me pray for them especially, Lord, simply because they, unlike so many

imprisoned others, choose not to turn to you.

I wonder what they were like as babies, as children.

I wonder where things began to go wrong for them.

I ask you to displace the evil in their hearts with love.

*I beg you for small miracles that some would
call rehabilitation.*

*When I was a child, the Monopoly game-board sent me
"to jail" many times.*

*My happy childhood prison-proofed me in many ways,
so I find myself praying now*

for those so far less fortunate than I,

*for those, but for the grace of God,
I would know as cellmate,*

*or fellow guest of the government in a place
they call "the joint."*

Redeem them, Lord, with the power of your love.

12. Leaders

Leadership and followership are correlative terms. When you are part of the followership, you should keep the leadership in mind when you turn to prayer. "Follow the leader" is a childhood game. Pray for the leader is an adult responsibility. But we tend not to give that responsibility much thought.

One way to stop a business leader, or any other kind of leader, in his or her tracks, say consultants Robert Goffee and Gareth Jones, is to ask: "Why Should Anyone Be Led by

You?" That question is the title of an article these observers wrote for the *Harvard Business Review* in 2001. "Without fail," say the authors, "the response is a sudden, stunned hush. All you can hear are knees knocking." Insecurity hiding, often, behind the shield of arrogance.

I was impressed about twenty years ago when I heard Dennis Goulet, of the University of Notre Dame, remark that to be effective, a leader had to be "available, accountable, and vulnerable." I thought then and continue to believe that these three qualities are uncommonly valuable for anyone courageous enough to adopt them as personal leadership characteristics.

Decades ago Dwight D. Eisenhower explained that, "the President does not lead by hitting people over the head. Any damn fool can do that....Leadership is by persuasion, education, and patience. It is long, slow, tough work."

Why should knees knock when a leader is asked, "Why should anyone be led by you?" If the so-called leader has specialized in unavailability, unaccountability, and presumed invulnerability, the question could be quite discomfiting. And any leader who doesn't see leadership as "long, slow, tough work" will surely be stopped or stunned by the question.

Whether or not they are willing to admit it, leaders need the support of our prayers. And we need both faith and humility to convince ourselves that prayer from us unimportant people for our leaders is important. How important? Let God decide; you just let yourself pray for them.

It is long, slow, tough work that leaders face, Lord,

made more difficult by the likes of me.

I don't pay much attention to leaders.

I don't much like being told what to do.

*But that's small-time leadership—on-the-job, local,
organizational.*

*World and national leaders are not giving me orders,
telling me what to do.*

*They come up with (and sometimes multiply) the rules,
but I tend to regard them as*

powerful persons removed from, and disinterested in, me.

That may be true, but I still should be praying for them.

*You choose to work your will through
human instruments, Lord,*

not all of whom are always up to the job.

*So I pray for them, that they may be instruments
of your peace,*

promoters of your justice, and stewards of your creation.

13. Followers

By way of modest commentary on his record of academic achievement, a friend of mine once remarked, "I was part of that all-important bottom half of the class that made the top half possible." Many of us can relate to that as we look back to our high school and college years. Looking at ourselves right now, however, most of us would do well to edit that quip to read: We are part of the indispensable pack of followers that make leadership possible!

You don't hear much talk about the burdens and responsibilities of followership, at least not to the degree that those challenges are applied to leadership. And when there are troubles at the top, we tend automatically to think of changing leadership rather than adjusting or energizing followership. Followers make leaders possible. Sometimes by default, often by inaction and neglect, occasionally by organized participation, the pack permits the power to move into the hands of those who lead.

The power to lead can be usurped and then it has to be defended against potential future usurpers. It can be handed down generation to generation through some chain of entitlement, and then it has to be explained by tradition or a rationale of royalty. Or the power to lead can be conferred democratically, by the will of the people, by the consent of the followership. The followers then can be seen for what they are: the ones who hold an empowering relationship. By willing it, they can confer or withdraw power. Their will is expressed by vote or consensus, but not without participation in a democratic process. And there's the rub: the responsibility on the part of the follower to participate, to be engaged, to remain informed.

So often followers are thought of as sheep—passive and slow, waiting to be led. Those of us who are not part of national, corporate, organizational, or governmental leadership, do not typically regard ourselves as passive and slow, waiting to be led. But we can stand convicted on that charge if we have nothing to present by way of evidence of participation in the process of organizational and political life through which leadership emerges. Moreover, the direction leadership takes—the issues and projects with which leadership grapples—is far too important to be left to the leaders.

I have a friend who habitually injects "follow me?" into his conversations; he punctuates his oral communication with this way of asking if his hearer understands, gets the point. He doesn't wait, of course, for an answer; he just keeps driving his point home. All of us should pause from time to time and imagine that those at the top or out in front of us are asking: "Do you follow me?" We'd be surprised, I suppose, if anyone in a position of leadership ever thought of doing that, but let's just pretend that the question is being asked.

This question, if you took it seriously, would imply that you are actively empowering your leader. Are you still there? Are you engaged? Your consciously being there, your remaining engaged, is important because your followership fuels the leader's leadership. This question would also imply that you know what is going on. Some people make things happen. Some people know what is happening. Most people have no idea at all as to what or why anything is happening. Responsible followers make things happen and know what is going on. Followers and followership are considerations to be taken to prayer.

"Follow me," is a familiar religious expression, Lord;

everyone, in one way or another, hears your invitation,
your call.

And those who write about organized religion
refer to us as "followers"

of one faith tradition or another,

allowing always for those who follow or adhere to none,

at least not yet.

I'm not thinking now of "following" in any
formal religious sense, Lord.

I'm thinking of followership as the warp and
woof of civic society, of

community, of societal life however loosely organized.

We need to stick together, we humans.

We have to surrender some autonomy if we are
going to stick together,

hold each other up, bear each other's burdens.

There is safety in numbers, the saying goes;
there is also a lot of wisdom

in the larger group of thinking followers who
make up the group.

So increase the wisdom in our numbers, Lord,

and give our numbers the push we need to participate,

and from our participation let leaders emerge

who are worthy of the masses of wonderful humans who are

ready and willing to be led.

∽

14. Winners

It is interesting to reflect on the way you react to the sound of the word *winner*. If it prompts you to think of luck—winning the lottery, for example—it is probable that you tend not to connect patient effort, or a long struggle, or persistent striving, with winning.

Taken in, as we often are, by the false conviction that the easy life is the happy life, many of us wait around to "win"—and that can be a very long wait—while passing up the opportunity to get started on the patient plodding that can lead to victory.

Some of us tend to divide the world into winners and losers. We admire the former and dismiss the latter as, well, losers! We want to line up with the winners. We hope their luck will somehow rub off on us. We separate ourselves from the losers because we don't want to be "like them," and we are oblivious to the fact that we all too readily see in ourselves the very failings we condemn in them. Better to live in a dream world of winners. Better to convince yourself that you (and those around you) are Number One. Give no thought at all to the possibility that your proper place is somewhere way down the line.

This optimistic self-ranking is, of course, not universal; nor is it all that bad. Too many tend to think of themselves as inadequate; so a little self-propelled boosterism can serve to shore up a sagging ego. Instead of being your own worst enemy, try being your own best friend—a winner. But don't lose touch with reality, which is another way of saying, "be (or become) humble." Be modest (and positive) in your estimate of yourself; be modest (and realistic) in the adulation you might feel toward winners.

Our cultural worship of winners ("hero worship" touches us all) explains the popularity of magazines and television programs that celebrate the rich and famous. Millions apparently want to read about the achievements of winners, even though this pastime inevitably makes the admirer more conscious (sometimes painfully aware) of his or her own shortcomings. For many, feeling good about winners makes them feel bad about themselves.

Grantland Rice once said, "Not that you won or lost—but how you played the game." The saying makes an important point: All of us are in the game. We need the winners to give us leadership, professional care, business development, scientific advancement. Winners are the rising tide that lifts all boats including our little kayaks and canoes, not just the yachts of the rich and famous. So pray for winners, for more of them, and for the welfare of the ones we already have.

Thank you, Lord, for gifting us with winners.

I know that winning isn't everything and that winning isn't always permanent.

But genuine wins move us forward as a human community.

I know that wins don't happen without winners

and winners arrive only after a lot of preparation and patient toil.

So bless us, Lord, with more wins and winners

as we battle disease, poverty, ignorance, tyranny, and so many other enemies.

Help us to see teachers, nurses, researchers, negotiators, and the legions

of others who are not in the spotlight or in the headlines, as winners.

Our forward progress depends on them and other committed and dedicated

individuals whose commitment and dedication do not depend on praise.

May they consider it sufficient recognition to be known by you, Lord,

And may they come to recognize that it is you

who prosper their works and reward them with your sustaining love.

I'd like to be a winner, Lord, on your terms and in the corner of this world where your providence has placed me.

Be the wind at my back, the firm ground beneath my feet.

*Help me remain on course, and give me the courage
to persevere, and thus become*

a winner.

15. Losers

I can't remember the first time I heard someone say, "He's a loser." I know it was long after I had come to associate the word with the short end of a contest, a place on the low side of a numerical score, a spot on the right-hand side of the W/L column. In settings completely apart from games and sporting events, the word "loser" is often applied to a person who comes up short in the game of life, someone who can be relied upon not to deliver the goods.

"He's a loser, a genuine loser," you hear someone say. And you pass that person by for a job, a promotion, a good assignment. Arm's length is too close; you distance yourself from losers.

Yet all of us know ourselves to be losers from time to time. Some of us think of ourselves as losers all the time. Maybe not you, my reader friend, but most of us know the experience of springing a leak in the inner psyche and seeing all the confidence drain out. When that happens, you hope that no one has noticed, so you hide behind a mask or remove yourself from circulation. And others may begin to notice that you are a bit louder than normal, a bit too talkative, overly critical perhaps—all the elements of "putting up a front" are there, even though you may not notice their presence.

There are very few of us who cannot secretly relate to losers because most of us have "been there" more than once. We know the feeling. So we should certainly know how much a bit of encouragement can help, not to mention how much "another chance" will be appreciated by those who are convinced that their last chance is now behind them.

It can be difficult for a person whose confidence tank is almost empty to be constantly reminded of the "success" of others. The winners are everywhere—looking out at you from your TV screen, smiling from the magazine advertisements, driving those nice cars that pass by as you stand there waiting for the bus. Isolated televiewing may help you kill time, but it does not put you in touch with run-of-the-mill residents of this planet like yourself. On the tube all you see are winners, young winners usually, at least they all appear to be younger, trimmer, and happier than you. It is not easy to be surrounded by "success." Loneliness and discouragement easily move in. That's just the way it is in the land of losers.

Praying for losers is a charitable exercise. It can also be therapeutic for the one who prays. No one is immune from loneliness and failure. How one handles these debilitating intruders separates the winners from the losers in the practice of life. If, as the saying goes, "practice makes perfect," prayer can be useful in getting the practice started. You can deal with loneliness and discouragement in prayer. By praying your way through them—that is, by finding God in your emptiness, indeed by permitting your emptiness to be filled by God—you can begin to look life in the eye and start putting one foot in front of the other on your way toward a realistic goal, a measurable achievement. Next thing you know, you've won!

⌁

*Lord, I find myself thinking often that you
must have great love for losers*

*because, as has often been remarked about others,
you've made so many of them.*

*You don't think of them as losers, I know, but that's how
they think of themselves.*

You know who they are.

*I'm just praying to remind you that they
really need your help.*

How do I know?

Because I've been there

in that hole,

all alone, or so I thought,

waiting for help to arrive.

"Chin up," I hear you say.

"Take courage; be stouthearted."

*I know that the remedy lies somewhere in my
willingness to put my trust in you.*

That remedy will work for all of those for whom
I now pray, if,

in answer to this prayer,

you help them, Lord, to see their need for you,

and give them the wisdom of letting you turn
their losses into wins.

From a loser to a Winner, is one way of describing
the route of this prayer.

From the eternal Winner to all of us losers will come
the victory for which we pray.

While praying for others here, Lord, I want also
to pray for myself.

Let me surprise myself from time to time
by recognizing that

there is no loser's noose around my neck.

I imagine it to be there.

I feel it tightening up at times.

But deeper down in my quiet moments I know
it really isn't there.

It's just me talking myself down, searching
for a towel to toss in.

Keep reminding me that I'm free to win,
at least to try to win.

The odds may be against me once in a while;
no surprise in that.

But I know the game of life is not rigged,
because you are the Lord of life

and would not have it any other way.

Handicaps are part of the game. I know mine and
can manage; nonetheless

I've got to stay in shape to compete in this game.

The fastest way to get out of shape, I've found,
is to talk loser talk

in the conversations I keep having with myself.

Let me invite you into those conversations now, Lord.

Convince me, if you will, of your presence in my life,

of your being with me all the time, every inch of the way.

Be my cheering section, Lord.

That's all I really need—your love and encouragement.

They are powerful enough to persuade me
that I'm no loser,

and neither are those many others for whom I now pray.

16. The Poor

Prayer for the poor can be an excuse, a labor-saving device that absolves those of us who are not poor from doing anything concrete to alleviate poverty. What are you doing for the poor? Praying for them, you say. Thanks, the poor might respond, but how about a job, or some in-kind assistance like shelter, food, clothing, healthcare?

When they walk toward you and look you in the eye and ask for help, you find interesting things to observe on the other side of the street. When the appeal arrives in the mail, you shoot for the wastebasket on the other side of the room. Your talk about giving at home or at the office may or may not be true; it can, however, be relied upon to shuttle you safely beyond the reach of an outstretched palm.

Praying for the poor is usually easier than doing something for the poor. This is no reason not to pray for the poor. It serves to remind, however, that the answer to your prayer may be a prompting from above to become an advocate for the poor, a helper to the poor, a benefactor of the poor, a friend of poor people whom you come to know by name.

Praying for the poor may be like throwing a forward pass to yourself. In your prayer you make the case; in your hands lies a partial remedy, your personal means, however limited, to contribute something—money, ideas, policies, jobs, programs, shelter, food, education—that can reduce or eliminate poverty. The answer to your prayer may depend on you! And that is why, I think, we often neglect to pray for the poor. We're afraid of the price that such prayer will impose on us.

Poverty is sustained deprivation. So you have to ask yourself: Deprived of what? Sustained by whom or what? What the poor don't have is easy to see—money, food, healthcare, health insurance, shelter, adequate apparel. What sustains those deprivations is not so obvious. Searching for answers to that question takes you up against systems—social, economic, and political systems that are populated by persons and help to explain why some have and others have not the necessities of life. Since you are somewhere in those systems, however minor your role, you have to wonder whether or not you are helping to sustain the poverty of others. That kind of pondering has a place in your prayer. The answers that emerge from that kind of prayerful pondering will point you toward a road that leads to action.

Some of the saints are famous for their poverty;

actual or spiritual poverty paved their way to heaven.

I know that, Lord.

Even so, it takes a lot of courage to pray to be poor
in any way, shape, or form.

Courage is not my strong suit.

I know that spiritual poverty—a certain detachment,

a refusal to be possessed by my possessions—
would be good for me.

I know how easy it is to measure people by what they
have, instead of by who they are.

I tend to think that way when I let what I have
hem me in, cut me off, keep

me away from sharing, giving, caring for
anyone but myself.

*I want to break away from all that, Lord, and
I ask that you let me begin now,*

by praying for the poor.

For those who have no home to call their own,

no money to meet their basic needs,

*no clothes to wear, no job to go to,
no education to speak of,*

*no energy for life, and no one like me to
befriend them, I pray.*

*You love the poor, Lord. You provide preferential
love and protection for the poor.*

*Just because I happen not to be poor, I must guard
against the mistake of*

concluding that you have no special love for me.

*Keep me mindful of the truth that I am the constant
object of your undying love.*

*And let that awareness move me to reach out to poor
people anywhere, knowing, as I do,*

*that I can find you in them, you who are everywhere,
are there waiting to be served*

in the poor.

Please, Lord, I beg for the grace not to hold back.

17. The Hungry

Hunger is the most urgent form of poverty. Hunger in the human family is a scandal, a disgrace, a problem that can be solved.

All of creation is a table set by God to meet the needs of men and women everywhere at all times. Everyone has a faith-based human right to be there. "For the promise that he would inherit the world did not come to Abraham or to his descendants through the law but through the righteousness of faith" (Rom 4:13). We the faithful are called to do what we can to make sure that all our brothers and sisters in the human community (broadly speaking, the descendants of Abraham) receive their share of the inheritance, have their place at the table, enjoy their portion of the meal.

That is the mission of the Washington, DC, advocacy group called *Bread for the World*, a faith-based lobby for the hungry poor. Advocacy is the *BFW* style. *BFW* members who, by their membership, participate in that mission are demonstrating their fidelity to the call to discipleship.

Members of the Washington, DC, Holy Trinity Catholic Church pass under an overhead sign as they leave church on Sundays that reminds them of the challenge of Matthew 25 by asking: "Lord, when did we see you hungry?" On Monday mornings they go back to work on Capitol Hill, in the White House, in law firms, trade associations, and lobbying organizations and find themselves wondering how, from those observation posts, they can "see" and do something for the hungry poor.

Those who grow discouraged in the face of mounting world hunger and poverty can find consolation in the Genesis 18 story of Abraham and Sarah welcoming the "three men" sent to them by the Lord. In particular, verse 14 of that 18th chapter is one that should be permitted to sink into the soul, roll around the mind like a mantra, and be internalized as a guiding principle and become a deeply-held conviction: "Is anything too wonderful for the Lord?" Cannot the Lord work any wonder? Is anything impossible for God? Yes, the Lord can work wonders. No, nothing is impossible for God. Why, then, does hunger still persist? Because, we have to admit, God chooses to work with human hands. And humanity's hands, including our own, have not applied themselves effectively to the task of eliminating hunger and balancing the worldwide scales of justice. We tolerate injustice. We permit poverty.

As I mentioned in the previous section, I think of poverty as "sustained deprivation." The poor are deprived of many things, food being one of them.

We don't know anything about the "three men" who visited Sarah and Abraham. Their mysterious presence in this story lets us speculate on the way God communicates with us, to ask who it might be today who carries God's messages to us, to wonder about the ways in which we might read God's will in the faces, words, and events surrounding us in the daily doings of life.

Bread for the World is, I'm convinced, an instrument of the Lord's peace. *BFW* raises a prophetic voice of justice speaking to power. *BFW* is working to reduce the barriers to the coming of the promised kingdom, which remains near, but not yet grasped.

We know that "whoever gives even a cup of cold water to one of these little ones" can look forward to a reward. So we keep in touch with the poor by offering cups of water. Even more important, we do what we can to apply intellect and political will to eradicate the causes of the hunger that is killing some and stunting the growth of others of our brothers and sisters in the human community.

Unless you are content simply to blame the victim, you have to look around for what might be causing the physical hunger and emotional weariness of those who suffer in our world. You have to try to identify the source of the burdens that are crushing the powerless. If the causes remain unattended, the weariness will persist, the hunger will kill, and the burdens will just grow heavier for those waiting to die.

The poor can't count on miracles. The hungry cannot eat promises. It is unlikely that angels will appear on the scene to ease their burdens. Humans helping humans is the way to go. Not the only way to go, say those who believe that miracles are indeed possible. But humans-helping-humans is a realistic way to go, given the fact that the "miracles" that happen in communities of good and faithful people seem to take a little longer these days.

Where better to begin working for a better world than by attending to hunger, the most urgent form of poverty? How better to address the challenge than by making a *BFW* kind of commitment to eliminating hunger through advocacy at those human, political decision points where the vulnerable poor can be helped or hurt. Meanwhile, don't forget to pray for those who have no idea where their next meal is coming from, and pray too for those who will have a meal, but not nearly enough to keep them going in the kind of life that we just take for granted.

━━

Lord, I'm not hungry in a literal, physical sense,
but I want to hunger for justice,

and I want to let that hunger drive me to do something
about injustice.

Widespread hunger is evidence of injustice
in the world that I inhabit.

Move me, Lord, to do something about it.

Nudge me in the direction of the needy.

Not that I'm asking to have my life turned around;

just let me make room in my day for doing
something—anything—to help,

and let me start by helping the hungry poor,

and let me begin right here with this prayer.

Help the hungry poor, Lord; you know them
and love them.

Do away with hunger in our world, Lord;
it is an evil that you despise.

Root out the causes of hunger; banish them forever.

As I pray, I find myself squirming, Lord.

I'm skipping a few steps, I know; quite a few.

*I can almost hear you saying to me that
you have given me the*

hands, heart, mind, and resources that,

*in combination with the hands, hearts, minds,
and resources of others,*

other persons and other nations,

can solve the problem of hunger in our world.

Why don't I use what I have to do what I can?

*Help me figure out an honest answer
to that question, Lord,*

And maybe things will change.

18. The Elderly

I am writing this on the 100th birthday of a Jesuit priest whose name is Jimmy Martin. One hundred years-old and all of us still call him "Jimmy!" An outstanding athlete as a young man, he turned down a major league baseball contract to join the Jesuits back in 1921, when he was just 19 years old. Jimmy Martin was also a star high school basketball player who, as a young missionary to the Philippines, introduced hundreds of Filipino schoolboys to that sport. He was in combat as an Army Air Corps chaplain in World War II and later served as athletic director at a few East Coast

Jesuit schools and colleges before going into retreat work in the Washington, DC, area.

When Fr. Martin turned 95, I remember telling him that, like most Jesuits I know, I look at my older brethren and find myself saying that, if and when I reach their age, I either want or don't want "to be like him." "I hope, Jimmy," I said, "that when I grow older, I can be just like you." In answer to the question everyone asked: "How do you get to be 95?" He replied: "It's easy, just work your way up to 94."

"Surely"—meaning "yes," "certainly," or "that's right"—is one of his characteristic and most frequent expressions. A positive outlook, erect posture, neat appearance, kind expression, attentive ear, and generous affirmation of younger friends—these are the things people notice about this old man.

Bob Hope was born on May 29, 1903. Over the course of a century, he put his stamp on vaudeville, the movies, radio, television, records, tapes, and compact disks. The Library of Congress gathered it all into a special exhibit, "Bob Hope and American Variety," in the summer of 2002. "When vaudeville died," Hope once remarked, "they put it in a box called television." When Bob Hope died in July 2003, the whole world sang, sadly but gratefully, "Thanks for the Memories," and no one has yet been able to find a box big enough to package all the laughs.

Variety is something all the elderly need. They make it on faith, hope, love, laughs, and affirmation (both given and received). How foolish the younger set is to look upon aging as a form of failure, as if the aged decided to give up and get old. Some do give up. All of us certainly get older by the day. Regrettably, all too few believe Browning's prediction that "the best is yet to be," but when you find one who does so believe, you have a gem.

My friend Diane Sherwood's career topped off when she was associate director of the Washington Interfaith Conference, an association of Protestants, Catholics, Jews, Hindus, Buddhists, Muslims, and interested others, who meet from time to time to pray for interreligious understanding and to work for peace and justice. When chemotherapy could do no more for Diane and she prepared to die, she organized with the help of friends a "celebration of life." "Let's not wait for the wake and funeral," she said, "let's do it now." And she told her friends, "I'm going to be just fine; you've got to stick together and make things better for yourselves after I'm gone." She died within a year of saying those words.

So we pray for the elderly that they may retain a positive outlook. We owe them so much. We are grateful for knowing and having them over the years and we hate ourselves for also being grateful that we are not old like them! Perhaps as we grow older, we will see the light.

Someone in a mismanaged municipality once quipped that due to a budgetary shortfall, the "light at the end of the tunnel" was turned off indefinitely. Not so in the well-managed mind and outlook of the positive elderly. So let yourself pray for the elderly you know, that they may stay the course and continue to see the light. As for the elderly you do not now know, pray for them too and look forward to meeting them in a better life to come.

∾

Inevitable and unavoidable, I know, is the process of growing old.

It is happening every day in and around me.

Although it hasn't bothered me all that much personally, Lord,

I'm remiss in not having prayed more for those who feel the weight of the years.

Perhaps I haven't been praying for them because I just want to avoid the issue of aging.

Or this could be another example of my insensitivity, my hardness of heart,

my facility for not seeing the needs of those around me.

The elderly are closer to you, Lord, in other ways than seniority;

I know I should be closer to them.

So let me pray now for the elderly,

especially those who cared for me at an earlier stage of their journey through life,

and even more especially for those who know loneliness now and feel abandoned.

Be present to them, Lord, as you are now to me.

Be their hope and strength, their light and joy.

And give them a fleeting glimpse now, Lord,
of the eternal dwelling place
you have prepared for them and all who love you.

∽

19. The Youthful

They are our hope, our delight, and sometimes the focus of our fears. The youthful. They are old enough to be responsible, if not fully self-reliant. They are young enough to represent a brimming potential for a wonderful life. They are well-informed, but not yet wise. They are daring, but not yet demonstrably courageous. They are on their way!

When I was teaching in the business school at Georgetown a young county police officer urged me to pass along this advise to male college students: "Turn that cap around, pull up your pants, and get a job!" Jobs are not immediate options for students who are not in academic trouble, nor are jobs their immediate concern. Even those who are serious about their studies, and most of them are, have time for fun. They tend not to be risk-averse. They take chances. They do foolish things.

At Camp Dudley in Westport, New York, those responsible for the summer program talk about "fun with a purpose." That's the way it ought to be for kids—lots of fun along with a deepening and developing sense of purpose.

A National Academy of Sciences report, issued in 2002, addressed concerns parents might have about traps that unsuspecting youngsters might encounter on the Internet:

"The years between pre-adolescence and late adolescence are often turbulent times, in which youth struggle to develop their own identities. They are eager to be heard, seen, and taken seriously, but often lack the experience and maturity to make responsible choices consistently. They test boundaries in developing their emerging adult personalities, and they take risks that adults would deem unwise. They are often socially uncertain, and they value peer approval highly. And in pre- and early adolescence, hormonal changes generally stimulate their interest in sexual matters. Because of the intensely personal nature of such matters (both sexual and social), the 'at a distance' nature of Internet communication and the anonymity with which one can seek out a great variety of information on the Internet is highly appealing to very social but also sensitive individuals."

Everyone is aware that youngsters know more about the Internet than their parents and spend far more time online than their elders do. Less well known, however, is the fact that young people go online more for health information than for shopping, chatting, or downloading music. There are technological tools to help a parent find where a youngster is going online, but privacy considerations and principles of positive parenting suggest that the most effective way to find out is simply to ask. As one observer noted, "Keeping a child out of harm's way on the Internet has as much to do with a parent's ability to talk openly with a child as it does with how computer savvy a parent is."

Talking with the young is, of course important, and it will always be a challenge. Recognizing their insecurities, their desire to be liked, their longing to belong in the company of their peers, parents, and other elders will be willing to wait patiently for the chance to get through with an encouraging word, an affirmative hug, a reassuring smile. They should also be willing to pray for the young who need their prayers.

St. Augustine's mother, Monica, is famous for her unceasing prayers for her errant son. A modern mother I know told me of her Monica experience of prayer over the years for a son who moved well into adulthood unconcerned about the damage that his out-of-control eating and drinking were doing to his diabetic condition. "I wouldn't give up," she told me. She found herself using the words of a popular song that amounted to a plea to God for help. Driving in silence to meet him to firm up arrangements he had finally made for a program of care that would meet his medical needs, she let that lyric prayer for help continue to echo in her mind. Idly, she reached over to turn on the car radio. And what did she hear? The very words and music that had been running through her mind!

"I took that to be an answer to my prayer," she told me. "I was sure that God was there with me in that car. I was certain that I had been heard and that all would be well. It was a moment I'll never forget."

∽

I tend always to think of you, Lord,
as being out there "on high,"

*although I try to remind myself that you are
also down here, in here, right here,
with me.*

*You are everywhere, I know, so it doesn't matter much
where I imagine you to be.*

*I reach out now to touch you in your every-where-ness and
beg you to protect the young.*

From their excesses, protect them, Lord.

From their exuberance, protect them, Lord.

*From their foolish risks, protect them without
hemming them in.*

*Help them always to help themselves to prepare
for their unknown future.*

*Hold them in your hands only to release them
to fly on high in realizing their potential.*

*Fill them with a holy confidence that will displace
any unworthy arrogance.*

*Encourage them to let go of selfishness in
exchange for service.*

*Teach them to distinguish lust from love, force
from fortitude, pride from simplicity,*

and always to choose the better part.

Freedom is your gift to them, Lord; happiness is their goal.

Guide them toward that goal in safety and security.

20. The Sick

"In sickness and in health," says the marriage-vow formula with a calm evenhandedness. Most of us regard the sickness side of that pact as a distant possibility, so remote that it is hardly worth thinking about.

All job seekers say their health is "excellent" when they submit a résumé and list references. Few think to ask those references for an assessment of the applicant's health. It is presumed to be good, if not excellent.

Despite the significant and growing portion of gross domestic product that is directed toward healthcare, we tend not to give sickness its due as we reflect on life in present circumstances and future possibilities. Most of us presume we will stay healthy although we insure ourselves against the costs associated with illness. And most of us pass hospitals on an almost daily basis without giving much thought to the problems of the patients confined within.

You don't have to be a masochist to see a positive dimension of illness; you just have to be a believer. It works best, I think, for the Christian. The Christian faith is rooted in a death and resurrection, an "ignominious death," as it is sometimes called, a death that followed upon freely-accepted suffering. Incalculable good came out of it all. Sickness today can, for the believer, participate in that good. But our present concern deals with praying for others, so we have to ask: Why pray for the sick?

It depends on the stages and circumstances of the illness. Recovery and a return to health is the primary aim in praying for the sick. We want them back again—in the family, on the job, back to school, out of the hospital. We pray for their return to good health.

But at times it will be evident that God has other plans.

I think of my friend Frank Sweeney, a physician and hospital administrator. At age 64, Frank knew he was awaiting death in a spacious room in the hospital he had managed for many years. When I visited him there and told him that just the day before I had been praying for him, together with a small group of his close friends, I thought it might be helpful to make the following point. "Frank," I said, "whenever we pray for the sick, we are always asking for more time. But someday, inevitably, for each one of us, the answer to that prayer is going to be, 'No. No more time, but how about eternity?'" And Frank Sweeney said to me, "My bags are packed."

When miracles are not likely, and when there is no longer any solid ground for hoping that medical science can work a cure, we should still pray that the person who is ill will have spiritual strength. We pray that the sick person will have courage. We pray that anxiety and loneliness will not weigh too heavily, that fear will be banished from the mind and heart of one, who, from a medical perspective, is now literally helpless. Our prayers can help. Our prayers express our love and concern.

We should also pray for the caring professionals who are with the sick in their need. And we want also to pray for the dear ones who stand by the sick person, who are themselves suffering at the sight of suffering, and find themselves confused and anxious at the prospect of losing one they love.

It is all part of life, sickness. Prayer for the sick, at any stage of any illness, is prayer that they may have life ever more abundantly.

∼

They need you, Lord, the Sufficiency for those who are no longer self-sufficient,

those who cannot restore themselves to health.

They need you, Lord, the Creator of all life, who in your wisdom chose illness as

a bridge to life eternal.

They can't cross that bridge without you, Lord.

Be with them in their distress.

Comfort them in their suffering.

Ease their pain.

Lift their spirits.

Raise their sights to the place you have prepared for them in a better life ahead.

Let me now pray by name for someone special who is ill.

Let me pray for sick others who are surely special to you,

but not all that well known to me.

I pray also for sick strangers whom I cannot see and will never know.

I only know that without your transforming power, sickness is no good at all.

Defend us all against it.

Deliver us from its grip.

Bring us all through sickness to a fuller share of life.

⌒

21. The Dying

To take the longest, most objective, and broadest possible view of dying as a part of life—as something that will touch all of us directly and personally—consider how a newborn infant has already begun to move toward death. In virtually every instance, it will be a very long journey, but the journey begins at birth.

However, when we think of "the dying," we look past the young, the healthy, the active and "productive" members of the human community, and focus instead on the terminally ill, on those in critical condition. For them, death is imminent, although their journey toward death began, in most cases, many years ago. As death draws near, they become poignantly aware of the unrepeatable onceness of life. This can make them sad. It is especially sad for those who, even if they could repeat their lives, would not want to change a thing.

There is a true story told of Helen Hayes, the late First Lady of the American Theater, and her husband, newspaperman and playwright Charles MacArthur. When they were young and poor, he bought a bag of peanuts, gave them to her with a flourish, and said, "I wish they were emeralds." When he was dying, he gave her an emerald bracelet and whispered, "I wish they were peanuts." The dying process provides perspective on what really counts in life.

Dying persons can be a source of wisdom and courage to others. Yet, awaiting death can be a lonely and frightening experience. That's why we should be with and pray for the dying. And we should not fail to ask them to pray for us when they finally go home to God.

I'm amused when I hear someone allude to the possibility of his or her own death by saying, "If anything ever happens to me." We just don't like to say flat out, "When I die." Imagine a lifetime when nothing ever "happens to me," absolutely nothing. Impossible and absurd. Something's happening every day, all the time. But we choose not to come to terms with our mortality and keep dancing around the certainty of death; we permit the "if" to distract us from the "when."

It is also amusing to hear someone who has recovered from surgery or an accident say, "I'm doing just fine—considering the alternative!" What's so awful about an alternative that delivers eternal happiness? Pray that those who are dying will get a glimpse of the promised glory and not lose heart in their struggle toward release from this life and entry into eternal life.

∼∼

Nobody wants to die, Lord, and you may or may not find that flattering.

The home you gave us here on earth is so good, and the people you have given us for

*family and friends are so wonderful, we don't want to
die and leave them all behind.*

You can take that as a compliment!

*And yet, leaving here means going home to you,
being welcomed into eternity by you.*

*Not so flattering to you, I guess, for me to resist
your invitation to occupy the place you have prepared
for me from all eternity. Sorry.*

*Thanks, but no thanks for now, I and others say
to the prospect of eternal life;*

we can wait.

*That's just the way we are, Lord, but that's
not news to you.*

Thanks for putting up with us.

*And thanks now for permitting me to break through my
earth-bound biases to pray*

for someone I know who is dying.

*I pray as well for those unknown to me who
are facing death this day.*

*Prepare their hearts as you ready their
eternal dwelling place.*

*Be with them in their loneliness, Lord,
be with them in their fright.*

Give them your hand to lead them home.

May theirs be peace, security, and joy with you forever.

22. The Dead

"He's joined the majority," said a long-time friend in response to my inquiry about an even older friend. I was unaware that the man had died—had "joined the majority." Try doing the arithmetic on that and you can't help but be impressed with the number of those who have gone on before us. Only God could begin to count them all!

"He rolled a seven" is the way a man I know typically conveys the news of someone's death. This is a colorful example of the "his-luck-ran-out" understanding of the meaning of death.

"Where's so-and-so these days?" I asked another friend. "He's dead; I really couldn't say where he is," was the tongue-in-cheek reply. Heaven is not a guaranteed destination. There is, we know, another fearsome alternative. Reason enough for turning to prayer.

An inscription on a mortuary chapel in a Jesuit cemetery reads: "Here the Society of Jesus cherishes, as keepsakes for heaven, the precious ashes of the dear sons she has brought forth."

Tombstones in any cemetery give names and dates, but little more. They serve as memory markers on sacred ground; they also offer quiet reminders to pray for the dead. How many cemeteries are called "Gate of Heaven"? How many of us are going to need some help in passing through that gate?

Why pray for the dead? The Christian explanation of this practice looks to life as something of a trial, a testing ground, a preparation stage for another life of total union with God. Some are not quite ready for this when they depart this world. We call them the "faithful departed," but they need a bit of help for the final leg of their journey of faith. We pray for their purification and subsequent union with God.

Throughout life, it is not necessarily God's choice to love one person more than another, although God's love is received in greater abundance by some than others, because some, through faith and grace, enlarge their capacity while here on earth to receive God's love. When we pray for anyone who had died, we are praying that they, by God's good grace, will have adequate capacity to receive the fullness of God's love.

All of life is aimed at love, explained by love, made for love. When we pray for the dead, we are praying that they will be purified sufficiently to give and receive love, without interruption, for all eternity.

Sin is a refusal to love. I haven't said much about sin up to this point in this book, but it is an underlying reality in any approach to prayer and religion. In fact, you can take the "lig" in religion, compare it with the "lig" in ligament, and then think of re-ligion as a kind of re-ligging, a reconnection, tying you back to God after you chose to break your ties through sin. When we pray for the dead, we are praying that the dead person's sins will be forgiven so that the person will be free of any obstacle that might block his or her approach to God.

⌒

I want to remember the dead, Lord,

and I want to do this first by reminding you
(as if you need to be reminded!)

of their need for your love.

*All of us need forgiveness, of course, and this
I beg of you for them.*

*I'm just using my voice and thoughts to
communicate their plea:*

Lord, have mercy.

*For their sins and sinfulness, their omissions
and forgetfulness, forgive them, Lord.*

*For the times they may have walked over others
and been oblivious*

to the damage they had done, forgive them, Lord.

*Pardon their unpaid debts, their refusals to forgive,
their selfishness and pride.*

Lord, have mercy.

Welcome them home.

Keep them close to you forever.

23. Those I'll Never Know, Until…

Some call the obituary columns the Irish comic strips. They are on the first page that those of a certain ethnic predisposition turn to when they pick up the morning paper. By definition, all the persons listed there are dead. Most of them are strangers to you. You probably cannot honestly say that you are looking forward to meeting them someday, but it will be interesting to make their acquaintance and learn more about their lives and achievements that are now embalmed on a page of cold print. Although you never knew them, you someday will, and you can pray for them now.

Looking through the rest of the newspaper, you see names and faces of others you do not know. Some are local. Some live in distant parts of your own or other lands. Some are famous; some lead relatively obscure lives that just happened to catch a reporter's eye. Black, white, male, female, young, old, rich, poor—representatives of all cultures, religions, language groups; they are and will remain unknown to you—until you meet them in the life to come. Pray now that you make it to that meeting. And pray that all of them will be there too.

You can and should, of course, pray to saints that you never knew, because they lived before your time. Pray as well to the saints you did know but who have not yet found their way into stained glass or onto pedestals in sacred space. Grandmothers, I suspect, dominate that population. There again, it will be interesting to meet for the first time or see again all these wonderful people in the next world, even though you have no immediate travel plans to get you there any time soon. But pause for a moment now to think of the joy you will have in their company!

I remember as a very young child being frightened at the thought of eternity. I can still see the green upholstery on the downstairs chair where my mother welcomed me into her arms and onto her lap when I fled my bed for the security and reassurance that only a mother can give. The notion of something never, ever coming to an end, was more than I could handle. It was probably a bedtime threat from my older brother that pushed me into a philosophical spiral that was much too heavy for me. But now I find it fascinating to think of an eternity of meeting so many interesting others, learning so much that I missed on this first time around, understanding every language, effortlessly absorbing the entire collection of the Library of Congress without turning a page!

All of us are locked hand in hand by a shared human nature. All of us are intended by God to live in eternal harmony with God after we exit this present life. But while here, it is up to us to strengthen our sense of solidarity with others, even though most of those others will remain unseen and unknown by us—until....You have to wonder whether eternity will itself be adequate to accommodate all the meeting, greeting, reacquainting, and rejoicing that are implied in all of this. Meanwhile, let yourself pray from time to time for the unknown others whose hearts and hands are just like yours!

∽

Lord, the wonder of it all!
So many, so much, so expansive a world.
Universe is beyond my ken, but within your grasp.
Give me a universal outlook when I pray.
Just being able to read these words sets me apart
from millions of others
who cannot read.

I pray that illiteracy will be overcome.

Just being sufficiently alert to think clear thoughts
sets me apart from

millions on the margins of existence who can think of
nothing but survival.

I pray that poverty and purposelessness will be overcome.

Just being strong enough to hold this book
sets me apart from millions who are ill.

I pray that disease will be overcome.

Just living in freedom sets me apart from millions.

I pray that injustice will be overcome.

I pray that the powerful will use their power well.

I pray that the intellectually gifted will unlock
the secrets of nature and

pave the way to human progress.

I pray for more beauty, creativity, and love in our world,

and I pray especially for those who are trying
to bring that about.

I pray that everyone will listen to his or her heart's
promptings toward goodness,

and that goodness will prevail over evil and carry all of us
home safely to you.

Well, there we are. This part has highlighted a lot of
"praying for others." Not too much, however, because pray-

ing for others carries with it an inexhaustible agenda. You may have noticed by now that there's something therapeutic in praying for others. Your own worries shrink to manageable proportions. Solidarity with others enlarges your outlook and shores up your sinking spirits. And I suspect that God, who created you along with all these others, cannot be anything but pleased to see you consciously inserting yourself into the marvelous mass of humanity in this unselfish way.

PART TWO

Praying for Special Needs

Any need that you take to prayer is special, but some are more special than others. Some needs are so widely shared that the entire nation is on its knees. Some needs are seen as family special, congregationally special, communitywide special, even worldwide special. The entire community focuses on the special need and turns to God for help.

This part takes a wide-lens perspective; it looks beyond the immediacy of personal need, although personal need is always part of the broader picture. That's just the way it is with peace, prosperity, and all the other categories of concern that constitute this present part.

If you can smile at the following observation, you're in good shape. If you see no humor in it, you'll need some help in connecting with the wider reality: "It's like magic," a shrewd observer remarked. "When you live by yourself, all your annoying habits are gone!"

Who, me? Could others ever possibly be annoyed with me? Sure they could, and you know it. Similarly, it can happen that when you pray by yourself and for yourself, all broader, wider needs may be out of sight and out of mind. That's neither good for you nor for the world. Responsible world citizenship, let alone a mature religious outlook, requires inclusive, open-minded, open-hearted prayer for all.

They tell the story of the jigsaw-puzzle picture of the world—the face of the earth—that a young boy was having difficulty assembling. Putting the pieces together was more than a puzzle to him; it was a genuine challenge until someone pointed out that on the reverse side of each piece was part of a picture of his own face. If he put himself together properly, he would have the world assembled properly as well. Turn that notion around and you might begin to understand that in praying for the needs of the world, you may well find that you are getting yourself together, preparing to have your own needs met.

24. Peace

The tranquility of right order is a classic definition of peace. If all the islands of tranquility in human hearts throughout the world were quilted together into one human mosaic, you would be looking at a representation of world peace. How wild a dream might that be? Corwin Edwards once noted, "Brotherhood is not so wild a dream as those who profit by postponing it pretend." National and personal arrogance, greed, injustice, and mistrust postpone, to the point of prevention, the arrival of peace. Arrogance is often linked to wealth, which, in turn, may have been accumulated by greed, protected by injustice, and surrounded with mistrust.

In the United States, it strains credulity for us to say, "In God We Trust," when our actions show that we prefer to put our trust in money, nuclear weapons, and unbreakable bolts on all our doors. As a Quaker and a pacifist, the late Steve Cary, retired vice president of Haverford College and long-time associate of the American Friends Service Committee, wrote a "Response to September Eleventh" in *Friends Journal* (March 2002), explaining his dissent from the view that we should wage a war on terrorism by taking a first strike at Iraq. "I think we should be troubled when we glance at our current budget: $340 billion for the power to kill; $6 billion for the power to lift the quality of life of the poor and dispossessed, on whose succor peace ultimately depends." If there is no relief of poverty, there will be no peace; this is the point he is making.

"Throughout history," Cary argues, "great powers and empires have always been tempted to go it alone, to pursue their own interests without regard for the interests of others. England was the victim of this mindset throughout the 19th century. In the 21st, are the immense wealth and power of the United States taking us down this road?" He sees evidence that we are taking that route in the stance the US takes toward the United Nations (not meeting our dues commitments, turning to the UN only when it suits our purposes). Additional evidence is our withdrawal from the Anti-Ballistic Missile Treaty, and our reneging on other negotiated agreements like the Kyoto agreement on global warming and the Nuclear Test Ban Treaty. "Blasting Osama bin Laden and his lieutenants from their caves or killing them on the run will satisfy the widespread desire for vengeance, but its price is too high and its contribution to easing the threat of terrorism too low. Destruction of a starving country and blowing up

Red Cross relief depots, hospitals, and residential areas—however unintentionally—only add to the anger that is the root cause of terrorism."

There is a distinction between pacifism and nonviolence. An honest pacifist needs absolute assurance that violence is necessary when employed in pursuit of a lasting peace. Your prayer for peace should include prayer for those on either side of the argument as well as for those on both sides of the battle lines.

You should also pray to preserve the peace whenever conflict threatens to erupt. Is that possible? Indeed it is. There can be negotiated settlements of conflicting views and interests. Just because a fist is formed is no indication that a punch must be thrown. Conflict resolution is another word for peacemaking. The late Jesuit theologian John Courtney Murray used to like to quote the Dominican Thomas Gilby's remark that "civilizations rest on men locked in argument." A good argument can contribute much to peace. Sound reasoning makes for good argument. Men and women "locked" in reasoned argument make civilization possible.

It is easy to bypass reasoned argument for mindless ideology. It is also certain that leaders who are caught up in hypocrisy, ambition, greed, and self-promotion will awaken echoes of this "word of the Lord" proclaimed by the prophet Jeremiah centuries ago, with direct implications for our present time: "For I will stretch forth my hand against those who dwell in this land, says the Lord. Small and great alike, all are greedy for gain; prophet and priest, all practice fraud.... 'Peace, peace!' they say, though there is no peace. They are odious; they have done abominable things, yet they are not at all ashamed, they know not how to blush. Hence they shall be among those who fall; in their time of punishment they shall go down, says the Lord" (6:12–15).

A sense of shame in the absence of peace is all we need to take us to prayer.

⌒

Lord, I hold the mirror up to myself once again
as I pray for peace.

Help me to notice the obstacles to peace that
lie hidden within myself.

May I have the courage to root them out and the
wisdom to see them as the obstacles

they are, not just to my tranquility, but to the larger need
for peace in our time.

I know that threat, bluster, and belligerence in the
human community have a way

of crowding you out,

but as I say that, I have to admit

that our blustering and belligerence crowd us out
and away from you;

we can never completely crowd you out.

You are always there—everywhere—always there for us,
and we're too blind to

notice you, too arrogant to listen to you, let alone hear
what you want to say to us.

Peace, peace, let there be peace in our world
and in our time, Lord.

May the gift of peace, like the gift of faith, be ours.

May the gift of peace, like the gift of faith,
transform our hearts.

May transformed hearts soon rule our world.

And may that rule become the reign that you call Kingdom.

It is possible, Lord. I believe it is. That's why
I pray—for peace.

25. Victory

Late on Saturday afternoons in the fall, as the football scores are announced over the air, I find myself thinking of the "varsity verb." One team does not simply "defeat" another. Rivals set out to "beat" each other, of course, but sportscasters use verbs like these in tracing the path to victory: A "downs" B; C "upends" D; E "sinks" F; G "trounces" H; I "edges" J; K "swamps" L; M "flattens" N; O "outlasts" P; Q "humbles" R; S "thumps" T; U "crushes" V; W "surprises" X; Y "rolls" over Z. Regardless of its color and imagery, the varsity verb has one target: Victory.

In sports, politics, and war, in any contest at all, the object is victory. Former Minnesota Senator Eugene McCarthy's sardonic and self-deprecating humor is still quoted in Washington gatherings: "Being a successful politician is like being a successful football coach," he once said. "You have to be smart enough to understand the game and dumb enough to think it's important." Not all would agree with that, of course, nor should they. Nor do most of us believe the piece of sideline wisdom that says, "Winning isn't the most important thing; it's the only thing!" The "only thing" that matters, our better judgment tells us, is "how we play the game."

Be careful when you pray for victory. Some victories are simply not worth praying for. Some wins are so trivial that they are not the kind of thing that should be brought to prayer. Moreover, praying to win can never pass as a substitute for working to win. Winning the lottery is unrelated to work and merit. Winning a scholarship is a reward for hard work. Winning a promotion or a better job is a fair return on your investment in education, training, dedicated work, and persistence. Winning the hand of the one you love is a gift of God's providence. You can figure out which wins are worth praying for, and which are better left to chance.

Every time I see the word "Victory" I think of the cover story in *Time* magazine that reported the end of the Second World War. That August 20, 1945, issue came to my attention many years later. It is worth a trip to the library and a search of the microfilm records to read it for yourself. Written without attribution of authorship (although I later learned that a very young James Agee wrote that story), *Time*'s report appeared under a three-tiered headline. The overarching headline was "Victory." The first subhead was "The Peace," and the next subhead was "The Bomb."

Victory was not something simply to be celebrated; it called for gratitude, of course, but also for prayerful pondering of the very profound consequences of the use of the bomb that brought this war to a sudden end. This victory ushered us (better thrust us) into the "Atomic Age" where the potential for both good and evil associated with the uses of atomic power bordered on the infinite. *Time* made careful note of "this terrible split in the fact that upon a people already so nearly drowned in materialism even in peacetime, the good uses of this power might easily bring disaster as prodigious as the evil....When the bomb split open the universe...it also revealed the oldest, simplest, commonest, most neglected and most important of facts: that each man is eternally and above all else responsible for his own soul, and in the terrible words of the Psalmist, that no man may deliver his brother, nor make agreement unto God for him."

All of our victories have to be examined in light of a simple question that can be expressed in several ways: In what way did this gain come at the expense of another's loss? Is it fair or unfair gain that constitutes this victory? Were the winner's points won within the rules? Was the loser fairly defeated or unjustly cheated? Where is honor in this victory?

The conclusion to be drawn from this line of reflection is this: Before you pray for victory, be sure that the contest is right, and fair, and just. You will be helped to make this judgment to the extent that you can honestly pray for the good of all contestants and especially for the ultimate well-being of your adversaries. The rest is in the hands of God.

*What price victory? Lord, I want to make this
an interrogative prayer.*

*I'm wondering where victory might be, what victory
might mean, cost, and demand.*

Can there be any victory at no cost?

If not, what price must I be prepared to pay?

*I know it depends on the contest and I'm trying now
to think not of my*

*petty battles, but only of the larger engagements
that challenge cities, nations,*

and worldwide communities of commitment.

*I pray for victories over crime, disease, hunger, ignorance,
poverty, addiction, greed,*

hatred, homelessness, joblessness.

*I'm having troubles seeing the faces of the enemy, Lord,
and I sure don't want to*

*make the mistake of seeing the enemy in the faces
of the victims of these afflictions.*

*Thank you for past victories, large and small,
that brought safety and security to*

*me personally and to the larger communities
to which I belong.*

Safety and security are precious gifts.

Deliver me from thanklessness in the face of victory, Lord.

*Deliver us—all of us in our nation and broader
communities—from pride in*

the wake of victory,

from fear in the face of threats to our security,

from complacency in the possession of freedom,

*and from that arrogance that could trick us into
trying to purchase victory*

at the price of honor.

⸺

26. Prosperity

There are those who firmly believe that a rising tide lifts all
boats, despite the evidence, in the midst of economic prosperity, that some small craft are beached or on the rocks and
other vessels have unplugged leaks. Praying for national
prosperity can, nonetheless, serve as prayer for personal
prosperity too.

As the tide of national material well-being rises, the
personal fortunes of the little people might be expected to
rise as well, notwithstanding the need to attend to those who
have no boats to call their own. Moreover, others who are
without boats may be clinging to life rafts that share in the
upward lift, but offer no long-term assurance of economic
security. Still a prayer for national prosperity is also a prayer
for individual security so long as the nation is willing to provide for those who (to stretch the metaphor another inch or
two) miss the boat that is being lifted by the rising tide.

Prosper is a nice verb to take to prayer, especially for
those who fear that there is something crass or unworthy in

praying for material gain. The final verse of the 90th Psalm repeats the petition two times: "Prosper the work of our hands! Prosper the work of our hands!" This psalm is said to be a prayer of Moses, so it has certainly stood the test of time. And if Moses could ask for a heavenly boost to earth-bound efforts, why shouldn't we?

Asking the Lord to prosper the work of millions of hands that are networked into a functioning national economy is an acknowledgment, first of all, of that nation's dependency on God. That, in itself, might be said to be the beginning of economic wisdom. Asking God's blessing on the work of human hands acknowledges another important point, namely, that the work is worth doing and the outcome of that effort will presumably be a worthy offering to God. Now these two considerations alone help first to establish that work is a vocation—the work is being done by one who acknowledges both a call from God and a dependency upon God. Second, if God "prospers" the work, then the material, tangible, salable, consumable product of the work is good, and the sum of all the "goods and services" produced in this way and representing what we call "prosperity," is also good.

Prosperity, however, can distract us from God. Our products can become idols. Idol worship is a problem older than Moses and one that remains to be solved in modern times. Golden calves now have wheels or wings. Idols may be real estate in exclusive neighborhoods, civic and academic honors, or business addresses and corporate titles that are the envy of those who are atheists by distraction. Smashing these idols is our responsibility and it can be done by the practice of humility.

Living and working gently provides protection against idolatry. Arrogance, personal or national, paves the way for idols to roll into our personal or national lives.

It cannot be said often enough that you have to beware of being possessed by your possessions. This is the point of the story of a depressed man who seeks his rabbi's advice on how to extricate himself from his unhappiness. The rabbi invites him to look out from the office window and to describe what he sees. He saw people walking up and down the street, young and older people on the move, scurrying about. Then the rabbi put the man in front of a mirror where, in response to the obvious inquiry, the fellow says that he sees only himself. With regret for having to compare him to these two kinds of glass—the clear glass of the window and the glass with silver coating that has become a mirror—the rabbi pointed out the need for this man to scrape away the silver in his life so that he can become less self-enclosed and begin to see others and reach out to help them as he did when he had fewer possessions and greater happiness.

This is not a "we-can't-live-with-it and we-cannot-live-without-it" situation. We can indeed live with prosperity and prosperity is indeed necessary for us personally and nationally if we are to enjoy life. (Nothing at all wrong with that!) So why not pray for the prosperity that God wills us to have?

Lord, I believe that you want me to prosper
and I also believe that I can prosper if my nation prospers,

so I pray for prosperity.

I'm praying for others as I pray for my nation to prosper.

*And I'm praying for my nation when I ask you to prosper
the work of my hands.*

Let prosperity blanket our land.

May farms and factories prosper.

May traders and merchants prosper.

May airlines and truckers prosper.

May planners, architects, and builders prosper.

May bankers and brokers prosper.

May scientists and engineers prosper.

May writers, editors, broadcasters, and publishers prosper.

*May lawyers, judges, physicians, nurses, dentists,
and surgeons prosper.*

*May scholarship, art, entertainment,
and human services prosper.*

May teachers, coaches, students, and athletes prosper.

*Let prosperity touch our stores, warehouses,
railroads, mines, ports,*

and every other nook and cranny of the economy.

Prosper the work of our hands!

∾

27. Success

Think of "success" now not in a narrow, personal sense, but take a wider view of that toward which your larger community, or any organizational or national unit to which you belong, strives: Success.

Here again, your personal success adds to the success of the nation, but your nation's success (as the success of any larger social unit with which you identify) also enhances yours. The point here is twofold: Think about praying for the success of the larger entity, and see an enlargement of yourself in the success of the larger unit to which you belong by virtue of blood, employment, membership, citizenship, or any other possible tie.

You may be recalling at the moment that "no man [or woman] is an island." You may not need to be reminded that the islands of tranquility to which your prayer may draw you are not isolation units. Even though you may be there "by yourself," as we say, you are not alone. You are part of a family, neighborhood, city, state, nation, world; you are part of a work community, a circle of friends, or a membership group that you must not forget to carry with you into prayer.

Quantitative measures abound when it comes to assessing the success of just about anything. Qualitative measures are harder to come by. What is the quality of the goods and services that move through the market to find their place in the statistics of gross national product in leading national economies? What is the quality of the life now lived to meet the modern measure of longer life expectancy? How high, how fast, how long, how much? There are answers for all these questions and the answers are typically taken to be measures of success. We are impressed with numbers, almost always large numbers allowing, of course, for those lower numbers associated with winning golf tournaments and horse races, although, even here, the lower scores or shorter times translate to higher purses for the winners.

At this moment in your personal reflection and at this juncture in this book, success has a place as a matter of special need. Success is survival for your community; survival is about as special as a need can be. But you should also think of it the other way around. If a family fails, if a nation fails, if any organization fails, people just like you suffer. In this very basic sense, a prayer for success is a prayer for survival. There are, of course, degrees of success. Just as stroke victims "succeed" in putting sentences together once again (that fall far short of stunning oratory), and survivors of car wrecks "succeed" when they begin to walk again (although they'll never run), organizational units can succeed without setting new records, without being Number One, without dominating all others in the field. Success has a lot to do with dignity, integrity, persistence, and playing by the rules of the game.

So a prayer for national success is a prayer for national integrity. A prayer to succeed is a prayer to meet a universal human need—the preservation of human dignity.

Be with us, Lord, in our struggle to succeed.

*We are struggling to survive with dignity when we
do our best to succeed.*

*I can speak only for myself, although I pray that
a larger "we" will also pray*

*with me for success without pride, or arrogance,
or complacency.*

*I don't want to be associated with any success that is not
somehow related to the service*

of my brothers and sisters in the human community.

*Although to succeed is to survive, survival alone is
not my goal, nor the goal of*

the larger entities wherein I have found my place.

Enlarge us all, Lord, through our collective success.

*Help us to experience unity in achieving success
in any undertaking.*

*Let us ward off failure by protecting and preserving
dignity in all we choose to do.*

28. Employment

It is so easy to think of "me" and "my job" when the topic
of employment turns up. Here again it is necessary to remind
you, my reader friend, that special needs are under consider-

ation in these pages, and that area, national, and international employment points to a need that should be brought to prayer.

I have often thought that the best possible social welfare program is a full employment economy. The work force in any nation is made up of those who are working or looking for work. However, in some parts of the world (and in some pockets of poverty in an advanced nation like our own), there are not only those who are too young or too old to work; there are the illiterate, uneducated, physically or mentally ill, malnourished, and otherwise unemployable people whose human dignity demands that they be carried by the rest of society. This is a societal responsibility. But, as I indicated, a full-employment economy is a necessary precondition if this responsibility is to be met. Prayer for full employment is a social responsibility of any individual pray-er, just as prayer for success in a job search is a personal responsibility of any job seeker.

Our everyday use of the word *work* is interesting. Something is "in the works." It will or will not "work out." Just go with "whatever works." Interesting, too, is our way of taking class divisions for granted by saying, "working class," and thinking of "workers" as those who toil in blue collars at the lower end of the job-classification levels. The dignity of work is often overlooked by those who see "workers" as laborers, and who attach dignity in the workplace only to higher levels of compensation. Dollars do indeed have a way of scrubbing up and making socially presentable those who do dirty and unpleasant tasks at higher pay. But it is a big mistake to let money become the measure of the dignity of work. It is money that explains the European visitor's observation about the American tendency to "tip the hat" when the physician approaches, but "tap the head" when the underpaid teacher passes by. Part of your prayer in the employment context should surely be for fair pay for all.

In the great Benedictine tradition of spirituality the maxim *Laborare est orare* is respected. "To work is to pray." Think of your workplace as an oratory. By simply willing it, your time there can become prayer for others. God can be found in your work and your workplace; and you need not be a monk to pull that off, just a person of faith with a quiet awareness of God's presence in your life.

In those familiar prayers of petition that we frequently make, there is always room for prayer for fellow workers, for those who report to you, those to whom you report, those who supply you with raw materials, memoranda, drawings, or ideas, and for those who will purchase the product of your labor. It is difficult to imagine that anyone who will read this book works or has worked in total isolation from others. It is not so difficult to imagine readers being accustomed to praying for no one but themselves when they take their work to prayer. Time now to make amends.

∽

I can't imagine a world without work, Lord,
not on this side of heaven at least.

I can imagine the hardship that idleness, joblessness,
unemployment can bring to

the world around me.

*It is a world of strangers to me, for the most part,
but a world of human strivers who*

*want to achieve, produce, make a difference, and,
in doing so, make a living.*

Help them all find work.

Bless their labors, Lord.

Let your creative power work through them.

*Let them be your hands in our world, the hands with
which you meet our needs.*

*Let their compensation be fair, their working conditions
safe, and what they do*

*through work be worthy of you and consistent
with their human dignity.*

Work is indeed your gift to us.

*May we use it wisely and well for our welfare
and the good of all.*

⌣⌣

29. Justice

A prayer for justice is a prayer for peace. Action on behalf of justice is work in the service of faith on the way to the achievement of peace.

There is legal justice, social justice, biblical justice—all are important, all worth praying for. Think of what a better world ours would be if all kept their promises, their com-

mitments, if all upheld their respective sides of every bar-
gain, if no contracts were ever broken, if all were true to
their word. What if fairness prevailed group to group
throughout society? What if social justice was the norm and
no persons or groups were shut out, put down, exploited,
marginalized? What if biblical justice—the condition of right
relationships, vertically with God, horizontally with each
other, and outwardly with the physical environment—were
the hallmark of human society? What if all men and women
were at all times just? What a world it would be!

Wrap your imagination around the notion of justice for
a few moments now. Images will help this process along.
There is, for instance, the image the prophet Amos employed
to communicate the idea of justice. You should know that
prophets are not those who, as the popular imagination por-
trays them, predict the future. Old Testament prophets like
Amos are those who point to the present injustice and warn
that if corrective action is not taken, dire consequences will
follow. Since more often than not, appropriate action was
not taken and the consequences followed, the prophet
became known as one who foretold the future (the dire consequences). Not so. The role of the prophet is being God's
voice in denouncing an evil and calling for remedial action,
and being God's finger in pointing to an existing injustice.
Listen then to the prophet Amos (7:7–9):

> This is what he showed me: the Lord was standing
> beside a wall built with a plumb line, with a
> plumb line in his hand.

> And the Lord said to me, "Amos, what do you see?"
>
> And I said, "A plumb line."
>
> Then the Lord said, "See, I am setting a plumb line in the midst of my people Israel; I will never again pass them by; the high places of Isaac shall be made desolate, and the sanctuaries of Israel shall be laid waste, and I will rise against the house of Jeroboam with the sword."

This is the famous image of the plumb bob. You sometimes see them in little holsters on the hips of surveyors. Although new technology means that they are used less frequently now, they are still employed by surveyors in staking out the lines and boundaries of new roads and other construction projects. The "plumb line" or, as we call it today, the plumb bob, drops directly down from the surveyor's fingers; it is a pointed, cone-like metal weight that seeks the earth's center. The string from the plumb bob to the fingers holding it creates a vertical line—a plumb line—to be seen in the cross hairs of the surveyor's instrument, the transit.

Israel is going to be measured for its uprightness, its justice, says the Lord, through the voice of Amos. If the nation is not upright, if it is "out of plumb," as builders would say, it will surely collapse. Think for a moment of how we borrow from the vocabulary of the building trades to communicate an idea of justice—"on the level," "fair and square," "up and up," "four square." An unjust society will fall just as surely as will a wall under construction that is not straight, that is "out of plumb." (And by extension, we have the familiar exhortation, usually from a father to a son, "Straighten up and fly right!" Or else!!)

Another useful image is water. Recall that water always seeks its own level. And think of the straightforwardness, the directness, of a waterfall. Listen again to Amos (5:24): "But let justice roll down like waters, and righteousness like an everflowing stream."

By far the best image of justice for purposes of communicating an understanding of justice is, in my opinion, the familiar scales of justice, the image of two trays in balance on a scale. You see that image everywhere.

Recall how the law is represented in the sculpted figure of a woman, tall and strong, a blindfold over her eyes, her arm extended straight in front of her, her right hand holding the scales of justice. The blindfold signals the law's impartiality to either side in a dispute. When the scales are even, justice prevails. When an unfair advantage is taken, it shows through as a downside gain taken at the expense of the upside loss.

Compensatory (*pensa* is the Latin word for weights) action is called for; the weights must be rearranged so as to bring the trays back into balance, into a state of justice. You see the scales of justice as insignia on lawyers' cuff links, tie clips, and other jewelry, on desk ornaments, wall hangings, and bookends.

In every application of this image the question is the same: Is one tray's favored downside weight taken at the expense of deprivation on the other tray? There must, of course, be some relatedness if the analysis is to conclude that corrective action is required in the name of justice. The relatedness between a pickpocket and his or her victim is clear. Not so clear is the relationship between advantaged and disadvantaged groups. To the extent that there is an identifiable relationship between the groups, then you can begin to look for evidence that one side's gain has indeed been taken (and is still being enjoyed) because of the other side's loss. If that is the case, there is a clear causal connection and justice calls for remedial action. It might be established, for instance, that the imbalance is the result of prejudice, exploitation, greed, or abuse of power.

Where imbalance is evident, but a relationship is not obvious and a causal relationship cannot be established, then charity, compassion, the common good, a commitment to solidarity and social responsibility will call for compensatory action that strict justice might not be able to compel. At times, appeal has to be made to our sense of humanity if action is to be taken to correct inhumane conditions or clear wrongs that have ambiguous or even contested social origins. The problem will not go away on its own. Even if the accusing finger can find no clear target, an honest social conscience will accept the verdict Rabbi Abraham Joshua Heschel once rendered in the face of massive social injustice, "Some are guilty; all are responsible." Widespread acceptance of that verdict means that some corrective action will certainly follow. It also means that prayer for justice is an obligation no person of faith can ignore. So, let yourself pray from time to time for justice.

Lord, let justice roll.

Let it roar down upon us like a waterfall.

Let it cover our cities, states, nation, world.

No harm can come from a flood of justice, only good.

*Is that what the Psalmist had in mind in declaring that
"only goodness and kindness will*

*follow me all the days of my life" because
"my shepherd is the Lord"?*

*I want to say that the Lord is my prophet who
will shepherd me toward justice.*

Raise up prophets in our midst now, Lord.

*Open our ears to their call for corrective action
in the face of unfair imbalances.*

*Rid us of that "ox gore" immobility that prompts us
to do nothing unless our*

particular ox is being gored.

*I pray for justice, Lord, because I fear that without it,
social structures and society itself*

will collapse like a wall that's out of plumb.

*And as I pray, I know that you might answer
my prayer with a suggestion*

*that I should act in some way, small or large,
to bring justice about.*

So in praying for justice, I also pray for the courage
to do what you would have me do.

Fair is fair. Let me know what I should do to help.

⌒⌒

30. Forgiveness

National forgiveness is something that we tend not to pray
for. Personal forgiveness is quite another story. We pray for
that all the time. But as we now look at broader, societal
needs, we have to think about forgiveness writ large. Our
nation should be our concern at the moment. Like ourselves
individually, it stands in need of forgiveness and it is that for
which we should now pray.

A Proclamation for a National Day of Prayer, issued by
President Abraham Lincoln in 1863, read in part: "And
insomuch as we know that by His divine law nations, like
individuals are subjected to punishments and chastisements
in this world, may we not justly fear that the awful calamity
of civil war which now desolates the land may be but a punishment inflicted upon us for our presumptuous sins, to the
needful end of our national reformation as a whole
people?...We have grown in numbers, wealth, and power as
no other nation has ever grown; but we have forgotten
God....It behooves us then, to humble ourselves before the
offended Power, to confess our national sins, and to pray for
clemency and forgiveness."

Two years earlier, on August 12, 1861, Lincoln called
for a "day of humiliation, prayer and fasting for all the

people of the nation." And this, for a people "afflicted with faction and civil war," was to be prayer "for the pardon of their past offences, and for a blessing upon their present and prospective action."

We readily admit that nobody's perfect, but we hesitate to admit, despite our allegiance to our country "right or wrong," that our nation can indeed be quite imperfect, morally flawed, and in need of forgiveness. Let your mind range over a long list of moral flaws in our nation, some supported by law and custom, others tolerated by a permissive society. Your list and mine might not be exactly the same. We will overlap here and there; there will be entries on one person's list that do not appear on another's. Collectively, if we are honest and, as Lincoln would have us be, humble, in the face of national failings, we will acknowledge a national need for God's forgiveness for our excesses, omissions, and wrongful actions.

Fast forwarding in our nation's history to the year 2000, the conscience of the nation was encouraged to look to forgiveness in another context—what the National Council of Churches saw as a moral obligation "to cancel the unsustainable international debt of highly indebted poor counties." Debt forgiveness became a widely discussed policy issue inspired by many faith communities' respect for the biblically-rooted notion of a "Jubilee Year," as well as by a troubled social conscience in wealthy nations in the face of debt repayment obligations that were impeding economic development in poor countries. Within the churches there was prayer for international debt forgiveness as well as prayer for divine forgiveness of those rich nations that refused to forgive debts owed to them by impoverished nations struggling to survive.

There is so much to think about when you begin to think of praying for national forgiveness.

Take an imaginative leave of your easy chair and let your inner eye rise high above the earth to look down not just on your own nation, but on the inequalities, unjust wars, hatreds, indignities, exploitations, and all other moral offenses around the world. Let the spectacle of all this move you to beg God's forgiveness for the hardness of human heart that produces conditions like these. You are looking at the world from God's point of view now, so feel the pain as God might feel it in the bodies and minds of those who suffer. See the struggles on the scale that God sees them. Make an act of faith in the healing power of divine forgiveness that can bring a wounded world into balance and back to its senses. And in considering the dimensions of the needed forgiveness, you can get a glimpse of the immeasurable dimensions of your forgiving God.

ᴗᴧ

Forgive us, Lord, all of us, especially those of us who are what we like to think of as

"one nation under God."

We have sinned.

We are sinning.

We stand in need of conversion.

*We need help in lowering our resistance to your
call to repentance.*

*We have to stop walking over one another;
we have to begin to see the same*

*human dignity under every color of skin,
behind every national tongue, within*

every set of national borders.

Forgiveness is your gift to us.

*It comes readily, unfailingly, but with the expectation
of improvement on our part.*

*So let us improve by the power of your grace,
which is, we know,*

a certain sign of the power of your forgiveness.

31. Recovery

Cover is one thing; recovery is quite another. The two are closely tied. We try to "cover up" potential embarrassments before they are noticed by others. We "uncover" leads to the solution of a crime. We are always anxious to "dis-cover" new ways of doing things (they've been there waiting for us to find them). And whenever we re-cover anything, it is something that was lost—health, a prized possession, poise, position. Our intention, once something that was lost is found, is not to conceal or cover it over (as "re-cover" would seem to say), but to celebrate.

When the economy turns down, we look for a recovery, a return to good times. When the surgery is over, the patient is taken to the recovery room where healing begins. Recovery always connotes victory, achievement, satisfaction.

You've heard someone referred to as a "recovering alcoholic." This is someone who once drank to excess and became dependent on alcohol, now abstains from alcoholic beverages, but knows that there is always the possibility of a return to the bottle. In all probability the road to recovery for that person stretched out over "12 Steps," even though the journey might have covered many miles of determined effort traveled for years with the help of friends. The heart of the recovery program is summarized in the famous Twelve Steps that are carved out of the experience of those who founded the movement known now worldwide as "Alcoholics Anonymous":

1. We admitted we were powerless over alcohol—that our lives had become unmanageable.
2. Came to believe that a Power greater than ourselves could restore us to sanity.
3. Made a decision to turn our will and our lives over to the care of God as we understood Him.
4. Made a searching and fearless moral inventory of ourselves.
5. Admitted to God, to ourselves, and to another human being the exact nature of our wrongs.
6. Were entirely ready to have God remove all these defects of character.

7. Humbly asked Him to remove our shortcomings.

8. Made a list of all persons we had harmed, and became willing to make amends to them all.

9. Made direct amends to such people wherever possible, except when to do so would injure them or others.

10. Continued to take personal inventory and when we were wrong promptly admitted it.

11. Sought through prayer and meditation to improve our conscious contact with God as we understood Him, praying only for knowledge of His will for us and the power to carry that out.

12. Having had a spiritual awakening as the result of these steps, we tried to carry this message to alcoholics and to practice these principles in all our affairs.

This twelve-step strategy works in countless other areas of addiction. There is strength in the human spirit—power to overcome captivity, to break out of the prison of powerlessness—and it all begins with humility. Personal recovery is a matter of supreme self-interest, a question of personal survival. Ironically, personal recovery can take root only in the ruins of personal pride, in the fertile ground of humility. And so it is with larger groups and nations as well. Lincoln was on to something important.

Now we have to think and pray about recovery from organizational and national addictions to destructive "substances" that we may not even recognize as being out there, ready to do us in.

⌐⌐

*Lord, we Americans like to think of ourselves
as citizens of the*

"richest and most powerful nation in the world."

We like that.

We prefer power to powerlessness every time.

*We admit in our better moments that power is
not necessarily force,*

*and we also recognize that power is not necessarily bad;
it is simply the ability*

*in our national life to move things forward or back,
up or down, or to remove*

things altogether—

especially obstacles.

Help us to use our power wisely.

*Help us to see in powerlessness the beginnings
of the recovery of all things good.*

*Your power, not ours, is all we need to move forward
not back, up not down.*

*Only you can remove the obstacles that block us
as a nation from the honorable*

pursuit of justice and peace.

Help us break all attachments to arrogance.

Lead us gently to humility, the state of mind where all
recovery begins.

∽

32. Courage

"Grace under pressure" is Ernest Hemingway's famous definition of courage. Any nation that locates itself "under God," as well as any person of faith in God, can relate to the "grace" part of that definition. Courage is a gift of God. Pressures of all kinds are experienced by nations and individuals, so pressure is certainly not unknown to individuals or larger communities, just experienced in different ways at different times. God's grace can enable little folks and large nations to withstand pressure. Indeed, in the absence of pressure, courage, like the diamond it really is, might not have been formed.

Sir James Matthew Barrie, the Scottish author and playwright, was on to something when he wrote: "Courage is the thing. All goes if courage goes." If you want a better appreciation of this idea, ask anyone who is battling cancer and who comes to see that the really "big C" is courage. Ask anyone who has had to face danger and survived to tell the story. If courage had not been his or her companion, the "live-to-tell-about-it" leg of the journey might never have been completed. All of this is easier to apply to individuals than to groups, organizations, and nations. But the focus in this chapter, my reader friend, is on our need to pray for needs far larger than ourselves.

An unknown author assembled these reflections on courage:

> It takes strength to be firm; it takes courage to be gentle.
>
> It takes strength to stand guard; it takes courage to let down your guard.
>
> It takes strength to conquer; it takes courage to surrender.
>
> It takes strength to be certain; it takes courage to have doubt.
>
> It takes strength to fit in; it takes courage to stand out.
>
> It takes strength to feel a friend's pain; it takes courage to feel your own pain.
>
> It takes strength to hide your own pains; it takes courage to show them.
>
> It takes strength to endure abuse; it takes courage to stop it.
>
> It takes strength to stand alone; it takes courage to lean on another.
>
> It takes strength to love; it takes courage to be loved.
>
> It takes strength to survive; it takes courage to live.

Substitute "courage" wherever "strength" appears in that lineup and you will be pleased with the fit in each instance. The value, however, of first associating courage, as the above list does, with gentleness, doubt, showing your pain, leaning on others, and letting yourself be loved, is this: Courage and humility belong together. Courage is a grace, a gift from an all-wise, all-powerful God who sees strength in humility. Just as earlier in this chapter your faith perspective got a glimpse of the power that lies hidden in powerlessness, so courage is now before your eye as strength conditioned by humility. If any of this is to be lifted out of individual, personal experience and applied to large organizations and nations—and you should be sure to pray that it will be so applied—the link with humility has to be made. Courage and humility belong together. Acceptance of this point is an insurance policy against arrogance in international affairs, an achievement that can come only by the grace of God, whose grace is the stuff of courage in any pressure situation at any time, anywhere in the world.

Perhaps *The Red Badge of Courage* came to mind as you began reflecting on courage a moment or two ago. Those who never read Stephen Crane's classic Civil War novel tend to associate red with blood, badge with honor, and courage with virtue. It isn't always that simple. There is a lot of irony in Crane's novel. Courage is complex. Like war, it can be quite confusing. Indeed, cowardice rather than courage seems to be the takeaway shared by most readers of *The Red Badge*. Just as "bad money can drive out good" in business affairs, so the memory of cowardice can displace the reality of courage, however fleeting its presence, during the most trying of times. Cowardice is a shameful secret to be guarded; courage is a gift to be cherished with gratitude. Let yourself pray now that courage might displace cowardice, and that courage always prevail in national and international affairs.

The Psalmist tells me to "take courage," to "be stouthearted," and "to wait" for you, Lord.

I'll take courage whenever it is offered.

Being stouthearted is fine by me,
if you will that for me, Lord.

And I'm more than willing to wait, but as I wait,
I want to pray for others—

for courage in my family, my community, my nation,
and in my world.

I also pray that cowardice be banished from the human
heart, from the heart of nations,

from the hearts of those who lead us.

As I pray, I can hear the voice of Hamlet saying,

"conscience doth make cowards of us all."

I surely want to leave room for conscience
in geopolitical affairs

and I think it can find its place without the
accompaniment of cowardice.

Discourage us from doing cowardly things in the
international arena, Lord.

Give us courage to do
the right thing, now and always.

33. A Solution

It seems that most of us are always praying for a solution to some problem or other, major or minor, but almost always personal. Now I want to point you toward praying for solutions on a far broader scale. The Israelis and Palestinians, for instance; will there ever be a solution to that problem or to any of the other problems in the Middle East? How about Northern Ireland? Where is the solution to the problem of terrorism? What is the solution to the problem of racial hatred and discrimination in its many forms?

Looking for a solution can be like bird-watching—somewhat detached—or it can be preparation for making a commitment to work to solve a problem. It can be disengaged and theoretical, or it can involve the searcher with real-life evidence and effects of the problem.

Do you think your way into taking action against a problem, or act your way into figuring out how best to take effective action? That's a pedagogical argument that will never be settled. But one thing is sure: We cannot afford not to think about how to solve problems because at times nothing is more practical than a really well-thought-out theory.

When I taught in the business school at Georgetown University, I had a very bright student who, immediately upon graduation, began working for a major business consulting firm. I recall thinking that my choice in consultants would be influenced by a generous supply of gray hair and evidence of at least fifteen or twenty years experience in the trenches. But this young man was bright and ready to go, confident that he knew more about information technology and its applications than men and women twice his age. His employer apparently agreed. After working as a consultant for about a year, he was asked to participate from time to time in his employer's effort to recruit recent college graduates into the consulting ranks. I asked him how he went about it and he sketched out for me a problem he would ask potential recruits to solve.

"There are a lot of left-handed people in the world," he would say, "and the telephone company is wondering if it can make life easier for them in airports and public places." (This was before the proliferation of cell phones, which appear to work just as well in either hand!) He would receive suggestions about redesigning phone booths and wall phones, rigging about one-tenth of the public phones in a way that favored the user's left-hand. Some came up with financial incentives to offset the inconvenience experienced by left-handed customers. I asked him how he would rank candidates based on their replies to this hypothetical problem. He said he was not impressed with their untested ideas; he preferred someone who thought it would be wise to start looking for a solution by asking left-handed people how the phone company could make things better for them.

Observing problems—looking at and listening for problems in search of a solution—is something that just about everyone could do more carefully and more frequently. Once we get into the habit of noting problems, especially large complex problems, we will be more likely to take them to prayer and much more convinced that only prayer can produce a solution. So let yourself pray for solutions. The morn-

ing paper or the evening news could provide the preparation
you need to begin praying along these lines.

⌒

Problems, problems everywhere, and no solutions in sight.

Where else can I turn, Lord, but to you?

I know you may choose to answer my prayer

with a nudge for me to attend to my part of the solution.

*So I declare myself ready to respond if you
just point the way,*

but big problems are bothering us now, Lord, on all sides.

*I can't do very much but pray to you, and wait for you,
and trust in you.*

It is your world, Lord, not mine.

You know it better and love it more than I do.

So why do I get upset and discouraged?

You're in charge. You know what to do.

You'll do it if enough of us ask you to.

*They call it "storming heaven" when people
pray in earnest.*

*If enough of us do, we'll come close to having the
"perfect storm."*

Let that happen, Lord.

*And let me see that in praying for solutions to
the really big problems,*

I'm praying for the peace, health, security, and salvation
that I want so badly for myself.

∼

34. A Cure

If word association were permitted to play freely as this paragraph opens up, "for cancer" would surely come to mind. Everyone hopes that we will come up with a cure for cancer in our time.

It is important to hope and to not lose hope, as the search for a cure goes on. It is also important that the search be driven by disciplined intellectual inquiry, persistent hard work, and adequate financial support. In praying for "a cure," we have to pray that well-trained minds apply themselves to the task, that generosity of spirit keeps them attached to the task and focused on the goal, and that both political and philanthropic commitment will be there to provide the necessary financial resources for, as we say, "as long as it takes" to find a cure.

It is important not to lose hope. And there lies a hint of how important prayer is when there is need for a cure. Hope is no real virtue at all unless things appear to be hopeless. Why hope for something you know is hidden somewhere within reach? "It is only when everything is hopeless that hope begins to be a strength at all," wrote G. K. Chesterton. "Like all the Christian virtues, it is as unreasonable as it is indispensable." Chesterton understood the paradox. The more hopeless the situation, the more hopeful must be the one in search of a solution. "Hope means hoping when things are hopeless, or it is no virtue at all....Hope is the power of being cheerful in circumstances which we know to be desperate....Exactly at the instant when hope ceases to be reasonable it begins to be useful" (*Heretics*, 1906).

Prayer is necessary to sustain hope; hope is indispensable in the quest for a cure.

Let your mind run in any direction at all as you fill in the blank: A cure for _____. The problem may be quite personal (addiction) or embarrassingly national (political corruption). You have to pray without ceasing for a cure for addiction, corruption, injustice, infidelity. You have to pray that bright young minds will open themselves up to education in languages, history, science, technology, diplomacy, and any one or several of the other arts and sciences in order to be prepared to participate in the search for a cure. You have to pray that the well-educated young not mistake the easy life for the happy life and turn their talents toward selfish pursuits instead of meeting genuine societal needs. This is what praying for a cure involves. Those committed to this kind of prayer will find themselves providing reinforcement for the necessary political will and philanthropic response to meet the inevitable financial demands that any search for any cure will make. Thus prayer becomes part of the practical response to large and vexing problems. And understood in this way, prayer is preparation, not a substitute, for action.

Cure me, Lord; cure us, Lord.

Make us whole.

Let us be free.

Only you can cure our nation of its ills.

*Only you can open my eyes to my personal
complicity in those ills.*

*Only you can give sufficient desire to human hearts,
skill to human hands, understanding*

*to human minds, to make them a match for the
problems that call for a cure.*

*Cure us, first of all, of our tendency to think
of you as a magician. when we turn to you*

for help.

*Make us mindful of the degree to which
a cure depends on us.*

*There are and will be times in personal experience when
the hard truth comes home with*

its fateful message that there is no cure.

That's when hope comes in.

*It comes in to partner with courage in sustaining the
human spirit.*

*There are parallel times in national and organizational
life when no cure is possible,*

short of a miracle.

When that time comes, I pray that I will
never give up on hope for a cure,

because you are my hope and I know you will
never give up on me.

✑

35. A Miracle

A miracle is not simply something that is difficult to do; a miracle is something that is impossible to do without suspending the laws of nature. No mere human can "work miracles," despite our readiness to attribute the power to perform miracles to outstanding quarterbacks, world-class surgeons, and masterful negotiators.

"We were praying for a miracle," you hear grateful parents say when a child recovers from a life-threatening illness. They did indeed pray, and the return to health is real. And it may most certainly have been a miracle that brought this about. We affirm it as a miracle when medical science can offer no other explanation for the miraculous result. When competent, objective, medical observers, after careful examination—before and after—of all the evidence, can point to no natural cause for the cure, the word "miracle" may be used. And when it is, only gratitude can follow, just as faith preceded the prayer that brought it about.

There is nothing wrong with the everyday hyperbole that we employ in assessing the dimensions of the challenge that a particular problem may pose in anticipation of a "miraculous" solution. Nothing short of a "miracle," we say, will solve the problem. And so we pray for divine intervention. The faith that conveys the prayer is all that we have to offer to reinforce the request. This faith can, we know, be so pleasing to God that, God willing, it will draw down divine power to meet the need, solve the problem, provide the cure. Hence, whenever we find ourselves looking for miraculous solutions, we should also be looking to the quality of the platform of faith that supports the prayerful request. Faith can falter. Faith can make long-term demands on patience. But faith, ultimately, is the only way we have of entrusting ourselves to God—no matter what.

So there you have another word that has to come into play when the mind thinks thoughts of miracles: Trust. Entrust yourself as well as your need to the Lord, who has the power to work miracles. You may ask yourself why so few miracles in these our days, as compared to the days and deeds of biblical times, and you may find yourself saying: There is just too little trust in our times; too little faith. Similarly, because so many deeply difficult problems can be solved by competent, persistent, and patient human effort—if only we had the collective will to work together toward a solution—you might fairly and wisely conclude that "miracles" are still possible, but because they depend on us, they take a bit more time!

So pray we must, and in praying for the miracle, we prepare ourselves to go the extra mile or two it takes to get to the cure.

Let me not think of you, Lord, as a "Miracle Worker,"

rather as one who loves me,

and wills nothing but the best for me,

and who will always be there for me.

There are so many problems that I see around me in the form of disease, disaster,

poverty, hunger, war, terrorism, and countless other manifestations of need that I have

no way of addressing, except through prayer, that I look to you for miraculous

intervention because no human solution seems possible.

Perhaps the miracle I am praying for is movement of human wills, human minds, human

hearts, and human hands in the direction of a solution, a remedy, a "miracle."

So let me simply say and pray to you, Lord, who are all powerful, that we await the

working of your power in our midst, and we are willing to move in whatever direction

your powerful providence draws us.

There are those who would say that widespread willingness to move among us would be a miracle in itself. And that indeed would be something well worth praying for!

PART THREE

Speaking about God with Others

36. In the Family

Faith-based families are a lot alike in their openness to bedtime prayer. Some spouses make it a point of praying aloud together before retiring. Parents "hear" the children's prayers before tucking them in. Mealtime prayer is also common. Although honored at times more in the breach than the observance, many families customarily pause for a moment of prayer before the evening meal.

"The Family That Prays Together Stays Together," was the slogan Father Patrick Peyton used by way of encouraging mid-20th century American Catholic families to adopt the practice of saying a "family rosary" every day.

But there is an important difference between praying aloud or praying together in the family, and talking about God and prayer in family conversations. To talk about God is more than repeating sayings and comparing images. Talking about God means digging deeper and searching for more understanding of the reality underlying the human conviction, yours or mine, that there is a God, that God in fact exists, and that the existing God exists with me and with

you in ways that can be described. It is in the description that
one's talk about God enriches the other, and vice versa.

Conversation about anything significant within the
family is often difficult and, in some families, quite rare. Communication about anything at all is a continuing challenge in
all aspects of marriage and family life. If it's there, the marriage grows stronger. If it's absent, so is the cement needed to
hold family relationships in place. Communication or conversation about God is the best cement of all.

In families where the spouses communicate openly and
well, there is still no assurance that intergenerational communication will be consistently good. Some adolescents seem
to be incapable of communicating at all with anyone more
than two or three years their senior. Whenever their elders are
present, they contribute "sounds of silence" at home and in
the family car. You can rapidly run out of questions when
any question you ask draws a monosyllabic reply.

Similarly, it is not always easy to bring grandparents
and in-laws into conversation with the rest of the household.
Sure, you've heard it before and you don't have to pretend
that you didn't; just smile and listen again. Yes, the hearing
goes (gets "harder") as the decades move along, and you just
have to remind yourself to speak louder.

Assuming, however, that conversation is possible, give
some thought now to how speaking about God might find
its way into family exchanges. In addition to conversations
about food, politics, movies, television shows, sports, and
the evening news, make room for the things of God in the
salad bowl of family talk. And try not to forget that listen-

ing together to God's word is great preparation for faith sharing. So is a faith-based conviction that God can speak to you through human voices at unexpected times. Be prepared to be surprised!

Spouse

Marriage ceremonies in the various faith traditions always focus on a promise, a solemn vow to be faithful in good times and bad and in all possible circumstances of sickness and health. The promise is a pledge to be with and for the other in a permanent relationship of love and care. It was summed up for me once by an elderly widow who repeated the words her husband had used sixty years earlier to propose marriage to her when she was just 17: "Will you have a conversation with me for the rest of your life?"

I think of that question when, through the rear-view mirror, I observe couples in their cars at a stoplight waiting for the signal to change. Typically, their lips are motionless. Maybe they are listening to the radio or a tape. Maybe not. Have they run out of things to talk about? What is the status and the quality of the "conversation" that launched their marriage? It well may be that they are so comfortably united in mind and heart that being with each other in silence is communication enough for that particular moment. Nothing is wrong. Nothing is missing. Or, perhaps they are bored with life and with one another. Perhaps they have just stopped working at keeping the conversation going.

A good place to begin rebuilding the conversation as well as opening up some talk about God and marriage spirituality, is to read aloud to one another the actual vow formula used in their wedding ceremony. It can be retrieved from books or the Internet, two sources of more good things to talk about than any couple could ever manage to cover in a lifetime of conversation. The "nuptial blessing" is another text to be pondered. All faith traditions have special texts that help to articulate the marriage commitment; any of those texts provides faith-sharing material for subsequent reflection by those who made the vows.

Returning for a moment to the front seat of the car where so much time is spent together, spouses should consider listening while they are in their car to a talk on tape or compact disk that explains some aspect of prayer, theology, spirituality—not just the spirituality of marriage but any topic that admits of theological reflection. There is always a lot to learn about religions that are not your own. Good tapes are available (even though a retail store called "Babbling Books" is no longer in business not far from where I live!); good books are everywhere within reach. If it is a tape or CD, both spouses just listen, and later talk over what they've heard. If it is a book, one spouse drives as the other reads, and the roles are reversed after a few hours on longer trips. Either tape or book can be interrupted at will for conversation prompted by the reflection just read or heard, and then the narrative can continue.

Reading aloud to each other can, of course, happen at home. It is something special for children to witness when their parents are attentive to one another, listening to ideas that stretch the mind, and sharing thoughts that deepen the love that binds them together.

Opening the conversation up to other couples in groups that meet for prayer and discussion is not at all a new idea, just an idea waiting to be tried in many circles of friends. Couples can grow together this way in faith and friendship.

The couple alone—just the two spouses—can use certain quiet-time signals as simple as the lighting of a candle to invite the exchange of God talk. Here's who God is for me at this stage in my life. What does God mean in your life? Where is God in our marriage? Where is God calling us to be, to do, at this stage in our married life? How has your idea of God matured over the years? Here's what I think of when I think of God.

In an environment of low lights and soft music, a couple can reflect together on the ages and stages of life and talk about the religious memories that surface, the times when one or both experienced the presence of God in his or her life.

If there is reluctance or refusal to exchange ideas in this way, do not presume that there is no faith. Just think of ways to fan those embers and let the flame of faith flicker up.

With it there will be more light on two souls, committed to becoming ever more considerate, loving, and free as genuine soul mates.

A uniquely valuable point of departure for any faith sharing between two or more people is Scripture, the inspired word of God. What are your favorite texts? What texts are special to your spouse? What does each text say to you, to your spouse? Talk about it.

When a circle of friends gathers for a structured experience of faith sharing, it helps to have a selected Scripture text on a page that is distributed to each participant. Let the text be read reverently. Let quiet time follow the reading. And then let anyone who is so moved, offer a reflection prompted by the reading and, after the reflection, simply lay the text page on the floor at his or her feet, thus signaling that the "floor is open" for anyone else's thoughts to be expressed aloud. If anyone at any time in the circle chooses not to offer reflections or a prayer, he or she can simply drop the page to the floor and the group is comfortable with the silence and not left to wonder if and when another is going to speak. This can work spouse-to-spouse as well as within a larger group. It can work within the family circle as well. Keep that possibility in mind as you read on.

Children

Talking to children about God begins in infancy and develops through stages marked notably by mealtime and bedtime prayers. There is a sense of wonder associated with a child's idea of God. Security is related to this if God is portrayed as a friend and protector who promises to be faithful, not as one who threatens to punish or reject a child forever.

Memorization of prayers, just as memorization of songs and sayings, is helpful for children. Very early on, children tend to hold hands and recite or sing prayerful words together. This is a point where a parent or teacher can encourage children to imagine themselves as so many links in a hand-holding ring that reaches around the world. An unseen God can be imagined to be somehow, somewhere at the center of the circle— looking out, listening, smiling. The hand being held on either side can be imagined by a given child as a small hand, big hand, young hand, old hand, black, white, or yellow hand, the hand of a soldier or sailor, the hand of a farmer or factory worker, the hand of an athlete or movie star. Any plausible pray-er, any-one at all who can be presumed to be open to God, can be imagined by the child to be present in the circle.

An atlas of the world in the lap of an adult can be used as a prayer book for page-turning children. Their minds can be stretched along lines of global consciousness and their hearts are opened in gratitude to the Creator of the world. They can be encouraged to pray for children less fortunate than they are and a sense of solidarity with those in distant lands can begin to root itself in their consciousness.

A family photograph album can become a prayer book, as can a school yearbook, an address book, a scrapbook, a family tree. Anything that can evoke memories of days past and loved ones who have left this world can stimulate prayerful reflection about their lives, their values, loves, dreams, disappointments, achievements, and, most of all, their faith. Sometimes letters saved can serve this purpose. Any kind of documentation of family history can be examined together in a prayer circle, not just with children, but with any family members of any age.

Words alone are not enough in talking about God or sharing faith-related ideas with young children. Drawing materials have to be at hand. Spoken words or lines on paper can provide surprise responses to the question: "What is God like?" It may be useful first to ask, "Who is God?"

However God talk is initiated with children, elders have to be ready to say who and what God is in their own lives as they listen to children speak of God in theirs. "What does God look like?" opens up a specifically Christian avenue of reflection that draws out (literally or figuratively) the implications of the Christian doctrine of the Incarnation. Ever so gently, children can be helped to see God suffering in human beings who suffer.

Talking about beautiful things is a great way to point to God as reflected in all things beautiful as well as to suggest that God is at work behind every sunrise and sunset, behind every blooming flower or flying bird. But birds fall and flowers fade; the earth quakes and skies grow dark. It is necessary to expect in God talk with children questions about evil, illness, war, and natural disasters that are theologically challenging to anyone engaged in an honest exploration of the question of what God is like.

Like true dialogue at any level, dialogues with children about spiritual things will produce growth on both sides of the conversation. Let yourself pray with your children and you will begin to notice growth in them and also in yourself.

Parents

The items listed above, like photo albums, letters saved, and yearbooks, can serve as special texts, not sacred, of course, but very special, that help to stimulate conversation about prayer with elderly parents. The challenge is to find both the right time and a congenial setting. Family bibles are especially helpful because sacramental records are often noted there and sometimes there are markings and underlined passages that bring the past right into the present.

To recall a baptism is to open the door to conversation about the meaning of baptism. The same is true with First Communion. Our understanding of these realities changes (that, after all, is what you should expect from theological reflection even on the part of amateurs) and the door is then open to talk (not arguments!) about new understandings. This is an opportunity for conversation about both God and prayer.

Crisis times are often times of prayer. Years after the crisis has passed, disclosing the content and direction of that prayer is a moving experience for those who are hearing about it for the first time. Elderly parents may never have told their adult children about the prayers they said for those same children when they were infants or toddlers, sick perhaps, or just growing up in a world of uncertainty, maybe even danger. Letters exchanged during wartime sometimes are revelatory in this way.

In a certain sense it is all about stories. Whether spouse-to-spouse, parents-to-children, younger parents (with or without their own offspring) to their parents, stories always enliven the exchange. Bible stories are always there to be retold. Stories about family life and family faith-experience are available to many and should not be permitted to fade from memory. "What is your favorite Bible story?" is always a good way to open up a conversation about God and prayer. "What were my favorites when I was young?" a child of any age can ask a parent.

Stories of economic hardship, probably unimaginable now for the adult child, but still fresh in the memory of the elder parent, open up opportunities for expressions of gratitude both to God and to the elders whose faith sustained them when their offspring had no idea of the deprivations and anxieties their parents had to manage. What child can ever fully appreciate the extent of parental sacrifice on his or her behalf? What child can begin to appreciate the sheer joy he or she brought into a parent's life? What a pity it is that these beautiful human realities so often remain unspoken and unshared! Just talking about them launches an exploration into the mysteries of God's providence and inevitably leads to a conversation about God and prayer.

This is as good a place as any to make the point that we can and should pray to (not just for, but to) family members and close friends who have died. They are "with the Lord." They continue to know us, love us, care about us. To talk things over with them in prayer is both a clarifying and a consoling experience. To experience God's action in our lives as a direct result of their intercessory prayer for us is nothing short of thrilling.

Relatives

Family gatherings typically occur around holiday time—holy days for many, special days for all. And when the family gathers, your "relatives" are there! Here's another word that is used in a variety of ways; comparing and contrasting the different ways can be instructive.

"Everything is relative," "it is all relative"—frequently heard comments like these suggest the absence of absolutes or the presence of cynical indifference. You just can't be sure of anything. Nothing's certain. Relativity, some would say, is an "out there" and abstract characteristic of our times that is a cause of cultural anxiety.

That line of thinking is not the one that draws you into a gathering of relatives, a family gathering of those related to you. If you stop to think about it, and look all the way back to Adam and Eve, we are all related to one another. We are all relatives. The personal pronoun "we" serves to remind that relatives are special, unique persons, human beings linked to you and you to them by blood or marriage. Tightly knit or loosely linked, we belong to one another. We are bonded. We are relatives.

Relation is, of course, a cognate term (I could have said, "related" term). We do speak of our "relations" when referring to family linkages. But "family relations" is more often used in therapeutic language about how family members get along with one another. "Relatives" works best to focus attention on real persons whose love and presence in our lives are enriching, or, sad to say, whose absence or enmity can be a source of sorrow. A network of relatives, some distant, some close, is part of your life. It can become a communications network for talk about God and prayer.

The relatives gather for weddings and funerals, baptisms and bar mitzvahs. Prayer is part of all of that. Family reunions bring relatives together on neutral ground—no declared religious purpose, just relating as relatives. In settings like these personal reminiscences can open hearts and minds to talk about God. Toasts and testimonials are usually part of these gatherings, so are spoken blessings. Relatives can help one another stay in touch with their faith traditions by letting that faith tradition provide the vocabulary for these reflections.

Gatherings of relatives generate their own special acoustics wherein questions can comfortably be asked: How do you understand God? When was God closest to you? Were there times when you doubted God's existence? Who in the family best embodied for you the presence of God, the providence of God? Over the years how has your idea of God changed? What do you think of when you think about death? What do you think of when a child is born and becomes a relative, a living part of our family?

Questions like these are a sure antidote to the nonchalant "it's all relative" dismissal of absolutes in our life. With beloved relatives gone, the conviction deepens that they are alive, well, and with God. They reflected God in our midst in the past; we must now reflect God in our circles of influence. God is the absolute in the network of relatives that is the family we know. God is there in the love we share. God is there in the forgiveness we hold out to one another.

What a rich source of reinforcement for family faith lies unexpressed in minds and hearts that timidly refuse to speak to related minds and hearts about the most important reality in their lives.

37. To Close Friends

Volumes have been written about friends and friendship. Since you were a child, it has been critically important for you to have friends—close friends, best friends, others your age who know you well and whom you know and trust.

Friendships endure over the years. Although not every friend you ever had is close to you today, friendship endures. Time slips by, the scenery shifts, the cast of characters changes. When an old friend steps into your life once again, lights go on, hearts grow warm, smiles reappear, and memories are exchanged.

Speaking to close friends about God is something we rarely do. Praying with close friends to God does happen at funerals and wakes, at weddings, and in both our religious and secular thanksgiving celebrations. But most would agree that speaking to friends about God doesn't happen often enough. Reticence on this point is sometimes mistaken for respect—respect for the privacy of your friend, respect for the deeply personal dimension of another's religious experience. But think of what both you and your friend might be missing by not talking to one another about the things of God.

In the presence of a true friend, you are free to say just about anything that comes to mind. The other is your friend, not your judge. To disclose to another how you discern the will of God, or how the hand of God may have touched you in a given circumstance, is privileged conversation. To hear similar disclosures from a friend is an enriching experience

for you. Whenever it happens, the fabric of the conversation
is notably different from the flip, friendly, but often banal
exchanges about pranks, embarrassing moments, achievements, risks, and those "good times" of days gone by.
Nothing wrong with any of that, of course, but there is so
much more waiting to be mined from the depths of a genuine
friendship.

More often than not those cherished friendships will
have common ground related to a shared faith commitment;
but not always. It really makes no difference as long as one
friend is willing to speak to another about faith or its
absence in his or her life.

Crossroads questions help to open up this kind of conversation between friends: When you left school, selected a
major in college, traveled abroad, went into the service, did
that volunteer work, started thinking seriously about marriage, took that job, made that career change, became a parent, encountered opposition, experienced failure, won that
award, became ill, enjoyed that notable success—the list of
possible openings is long. When whatever it was—good or
bad—that happened to you, my friend, where was God? Let
me tell you, you might say, about my crossroad quandaries,
my answers to the boundary questions in my life, my experience of God in times of crisis and consolation.

Only you (and your friends) can write the book (or
notebook) on these themes. Something of a "writers' work-
shop" can happen in the atmosphere of trust and desire to
talk about the past that characterizes friendship at its best.
You have to set the table, so to speak, if you are going to

enjoy some table talk together. You have to ask. You have to be willing to answer.

One friend asked another who was in-between jobs—looking, but not yet reemployed—how he was doing and how God fit into his life and his job search. "I do not believe that God necessarily has an interest in the quality of my next job," replied the job seeker. "I know that God loves me and has given me a mix of talents and challenges and it is up to me to make it all work. I may very well pray for a certain outcome, but in my heart I know that the prayer is more to maintain an ongoing conversation than to request a specific outcome. While I do not expect God to intervene in my job search, I do not feel abandoned. My spiritual life should not suffer whether my next job is as a janitor or as a CEO. I will certainly try to end up more toward the CEO-end of the spectrum, but that is irrelevant to my relationship with God."

The important thing, both friends agreed, was to have that "ongoing conversation" with God in prayer.

38. In Time of Illness

Any illness is an interruption to ordinary routine. Any illness sets you back, makes you think, offers a reminder—to those open to the suggestion—that you are mortal, less than perfect, not always in control. Any illness can therefore be an occasion for prayer. The prayer might be for recovery, for endurance in suffering, for resignation to the will of God, or for a combination of all three. The illness can also occasion talk about God with those whose presence to you in your need brings comfort and reassurance.

Serious illness can also bring about an argument, within yourself or between you and those who try to comfort you, about the whereabouts of God in your moment of need and the involvement of God in your present distress. Did God make you ill, somehow cause your illness? Is God punishing you with this affliction? How can an all-good, all-loving, all-powerful God stand by and do nothing to help you? Is there any meaning at all to be found in the experience of human suffering? Does any of this unpleasant experience make sense in the context of a human life?

Questions like these are asked and answered every day in the lives of ordinary people. The point at this stage of our shared reflection, my reader friend, is simply to consider how any of us might speak of God with others when we or they are ill.

It can begin easily and naturally with a touch of the hand. The hand of the caregiver, the visitor, the faithful family member who is standing by the person who is ill, establishes a special presence as if to say, "I am here with you, and for you, and God is with us both."

"God be with you," as we all know, enunciates in our vernacular, "God be wi' ye" or "goodbye." The visitor is, however, saying to the sick person, "Hello, I am here, and God is here with us both." Hand upon hand, voice to voice, friend to friend, soul to soul. It is not yet goodbye, although that may soon be all there is to say. For the person who is seriously ill, the presence of God is cradled in the hand whose touch conveys without words that special presence.

An invitation to pray together is welcomed in that setting. Repetition of familiar prayers, long ago committed to memory, can be consoling and strengthening in these moments. The person who is well can read a psalm or a familiar passage from Scripture; and appropriate reflections or favorite sayings can be read. But excessive words are never helpful; the healing power of silent prayer is often overlooked.

Conversation about the God to whom the prayer is addressed is natural at this time, just as talk about the saints and angels whose intercession might be invoked to accompany those prayers is also congenial to those whose hands are locked and whose faith is shared.

Naturally, the person who is ill will want to hear news about family members and friends who are not present. Talk about people (even about pets!) is always an important component of the visit. But it is all too easy to substitute talk about trivialities for talk about God. And although family and friends are certainly not trivial, there is within us all a curious inhibitor that holds us back from speaking aloud about the presence of God in the very persons we hold so dear.

Before Surgery

There is no surgery, of course, without a surgeon. He or she may or may not be a person of faith. No need to talk to your surgeon about God before the operation, but it is always a great idea to talk to God about your surgeon before the procedure gets underway! Pray that God will guide the surgeon's hand and bless him or her with good judgment.

God's healing power works through the wonderful but ordinary means of human hands, eyes, and decisions.

Any pre-operative prayer by the patient or by those who are praying for the success of the surgery, should always include prayer for the surgeon. Understandably, the preoccupation of the patient will be on him- or herself. Regardless of who prays, pre-operative prayer will always be for what the medical personnel like to call a "good result" and what patients and their loved ones look upon as a "happy outcome." But surgery provides a context for a profoundly personal prayer experience as well, and a richly theological conversation between and among persons of faith about God.

Faith is the act by which you entrust yourself to God. Much, much more could be said about faith, of course, but the notion of trust is all we need to begin talking about God in the context of surgery. Anyone who has been through it knows how helplessness underlies the pain or trauma that has brought the person into surgery. Even if you could, you would never want to perform surgery on yourself. You entrust yourself to the surgeon's care. You find yourself thinking or saying that you have "faith" in your surgeon. It is not divine faith, of course, but it is genuine trust. Reflection on that trust can provide for you a faint glimmer of the beauty and strength of the trust you place in God through your act of faith.

Supernatural faith is a reality in your life that you talk about all too infrequently. Surgery, in all its before-and-after stages, provides a privileged platform for serious talk about supernatural faith. Paul's Second Letter to the

Corinthians says it so well: "We walk by faith and not by sight" (2 Cor 5:7).

You cannot see the future. You cannot see the direction in which your marriage or career will move. You cannot see the circumstances that will surround your children's growth to maturity. You cannot see your medical future. And yet you walk. You walk confidently (the word, if I may remind you once again, means "with faith"). You walk hopefully toward a promised future, a future that you know is there because you have the promise. You are a person of faith. Even though you have perfect vision (and are unqualifiedly grateful that you have), you do not walk "by sight."

You walk by faith all the time, not just in those troubled times that bring you to a point where you put your life in the hands of a surgeon. The experience of doing that, however, and the euphoria that is yours in function of the "good result," give you something to talk about with friends and family who share your faith convictions. After giving surgeons, medical science, wonder drugs, and the wonder workers of the healthcare system all the credit they so richly deserve, you cannot ignore the evidence of surgical failures and even malpractice. So if your faith is so great in the this-world reality of medical miracles (and justifiably so), how much greater should it be in the other-world reality of divine power and forgiveness?

Don't bore us with details about your operation. Just encourage us with talk about the power of the hand of God behind the hand of your surgeon!

During Chronic Illness

Time is a silent, stolid presence surrounding those who are chronically ill. It moves ever so slowly. As time passes, week by week, month by month, year into year, talking to a chronically ill person about God becomes progressively more challenging. For persons of faith, silence without surrender will come to characterize the conversation for lengthening intervals. Faith can turn stoic endurance into patient acceptance as prospects for a return to health remain remote.

Talking about God to and with a person whose illness shows no sign of abatement is a great gift to the sick person. Some will request it. Others will welcome it when it comes. Few, if any, will resent it, so long as it is a quiet communication free of exhortation and any hint of an effort to persuade or convert.

A motto, a cherished saying, a familiar mantra can help sustain the spirit during a long illness. Helping the patient mine his or her memory for helpful sayings is an excellent way to get a conversation going that leads to talk about God. Once the words are there, repeating them is helpful and reducing them to print for easy reference is a welcome gift. Words like these, often attributed to St. Francis of Assisi, are always welcome: "Lord, give me the strength to change the things I must change, the courage to bear the things I cannot change, and the wisdom to know the difference." Thomas Fuller put the same thought another way: "What cannot be altered must be borne, not blamed." How helpful it is to remove blame from the picture altogether!

Having something—anything at all—to talk about is an important precondition for a good conversation with a long-term patient. Be prepared. Make points for the conversation. Remember what was said in recent conversations; plan to cover this or that in future conversations. Otherwise, in addition to awkward silences, it will be the weather and other topics of no particular interest or importance.

Poetry can be particularly useful in these situations. Curious, isn't it, how poetry, which is not written to be practical, can be useful in centering down on words and ideas that have the practical effect of staying with a sick person over time. Search anywhere you like for poetry that works in this way.

Wordsworth frames the challenge of endurance in terms of love: "There is a comfort in the strength of love;/ 'Twill make a thing endurable, which else/ Would overset the brain, or break the heart." Practical comfort might be drawn from Shakespeare's line in *Henry V*: "Though patience be a tired mare, yet she will plod." Almost by definition, chronic illness means always being tired. Admit it, and plod on.

The length-of-stay of any chronic illness is, by definition, long. The longer it gets, the greater is the temptation for a patient to devalue his or her present status because he or she is no longer able to "do" as in the past. Not to do, for all too many people, is not to be. It is, therefore, crucially important for the conversation about God to begin with an acknowledgment that being is infinitely more important than doing, that being for the believer is forever, and that the source of all being is God. Turning to God means returning to the source of one's being. To reflect on this is to think philosophically and to philosophize is to ask and answer questions. The chronically ill patient has the time to do this, but may not have the inclination. What is needed is a patient friend—that is, not another sick person who is a friend, but a friend who is patient—who has both the inclination and the time to let the dialogue begin.

How, you might ask the person who is ill, might St. Paul's words to the Romans (5:3–5) apply to you in these circumstances of chronic illness? "[W]e boast in hope of the glory of God. Not only that, but we even boast of our afflictions, knowing that afflictions produce endurance, and endurance, proven character, and proven character, hope, and hope does not disappoint, because the love of God has been poured out into our hearts through the Holy Spirit that has been given to us."

Hope enables a believer to be cheerful in circumstances that provide no cause for joy. And the direct object of one's supernatural hope is, of course, God. Now there is something surely worth talking about.

During Recovery

Gratitude, as I've mentioned several times earlier in this book, is the cornerstone of religious experience. In any circumstance, not just the situation of illness and recovery, gratitude is the infrastructure underlying all awareness the believer has of the things of God.

For the surgical patient, gratitude begins in the recovery room and grows throughout the process of recovery.

What will have been recovered at the end of this process is, of course, good health manifested in restored mobility, freedom from pain, regained ability to function.

Recovery also reintroduces the idea of patience-as-a-virtue to the person who continues to be a-patient-under-care. Patience is a challenge for every patient. Many demonstrate behavior that contradicts the label they bear; they are anything but patient. The impatient patient is not really a contradiction in terms, just a nuisance to those responsible for the recovery process. It can be gently pointed out by anyone brave enough to open up some talk about God in this kind of situation, that an impatient patient is also an ingrate.

"Thank God," say friends and family members to recovering patients and to themselves. "Thank God" should become a very personal and profound, "Thank you, Lord," on the lips of the recovering patient. "How great thou art!" How grateful am I, you should be saying to yourself, as you think and talk once more about the future.

Recovery time should become quite literally strategic planning time. This is an opportunity to be talking about God as well as making prayer part of the planning process.

What's ahead? What's my goal? How am I planning to get there? What adjustments will have to be made? Any losses to be recouped? Any need to rearrange priorities on my personal scale of what's important?

Strategic planning begins with strategic thinking, and strategic thinking begins with questions like these. But the first question to be answered by the individual planner (just as it would be for an organization or corporation) is: What sets me apart? I've got to build my plan on my comparative advantage. I'm a bit different now. Part of me has been surgically removed or repaired. I've endured a process; I've been through something that has had an impact that I can quite literally feel, but may not yet understand. What is it now that sets me apart?

The patient-planner needs to talk these questions out with a trusted friend, an adviser, a spouse, a mentor. It would be the height of ingratitude to let that conversation proceed without any word to, or about, God. It would be a practical blasphemy to have sought God's help in illness and then turn away from (or even against) God on a path to recovery that stretches out to destinations that are distant from the love of God.

The vocabulary of stewardship, familiar to many religious traditions, is useful for talking about and praying to God during recovery. Stewards are managers, not owners. The experience of illness serves to remind that we do not really own our bodies and minds. They are gifts that we have to manage. We use them for God's glory and the good of others, for the service of our brothers and sisters in the human community. And in using these gifts we find happiness.

Stewardship over these gifts is a personal responsibility. At times, our failure to exercise responsible stewardship, leads to damaged health. We all know about the importance of proper diet, exercise, rest, and the avoidance or abuse of certain addictive substances. Good stewards attend to these matters. Failure to do so leads to illness.

Recovery from illness is planning time for a stewardship strategy that recognizes God as owner and the recovering patients as persons who hold a significant portion of their medical destinies in their own hands. How are you now going to give praise and thanks to God by managing carefully the assets of the mind and body that are God's gift to you? Discussing that question inevitably involves talking about God. Praying about that question is integral to the recovery process.

Those who believe in divine forgiveness know that they live in a world of second chances. Fresh starts, new beginnings are always possible, even when the sun has set and darkness is descending. That's the way it always is for people who place their hope in God!

39. In Time of Sorrow

"Sorry for your troubles," say the Irish at wakes and funerals. Survivors of the deceased are the ones who have more cause for sorrow, of course, but they appreciate the "trouble" others take to come and "pay their respects." Trouble and sorrow are closely linked in the Irish experience, as they are just about anywhere else in the world.

In time of sorrow, talking about God will almost certainly help, but it isn't always easy to begin. That is why we ritualize expressions of sorrow at wakes and funerals. That's why we send flowers. That's why note card manufacturers print sayings like "A sorrow shared is a sorrow halved" and those who want to can scribble expressions of sympathy on the back of the card. The Greek word *sun-pathein* becomes "sympathy" in English. It means "with suffering," or better, "suffering with" another, getting somehow inside the other's suffering, sharing the experience of another's sorrow. Very, very hard to do. But because we care, we want to try.

"Leave me alone" is sometimes the honest but unexpressed reaction of the sorrowing person. "Just remain here with me," or, "Hold me," can be the soulful wish of others. You never know until you get close enough to read what is in the heart of the other. Friendship or kinship gives you the right to be there; nothing but love and knowledge of the other can prepare you to make the correct reading. Once you begin to speak, you will know. Beginning to speak is easier if your speech is of and about God. Cowardice can prevent you from saying anything, or even from being there in the first place, but cowardice can always be overcome by grace.

Faith traditions divide along lines of how they deal with loss, death, sorrow, and separation. Hence there is no one-size-fits-all talk about God in the context of sorrow, no matter how that sorrow may have been triggered, whatever its cause. Praying with a sorrowing person will also vary by faith tradition. However, the religions that express those respective faiths provide the words that can help the prayer begin.

Being with and being there for the other in a time of sorrow is the important thing. The words will come; and the words will be right when they come.

Death

Karl Rahner spoke of the "unrepeatable onceness" of life that is made so strikingly clear by the fact of death. This points to one of two fundamental directions in which the conversation can move when you want to talk about God in the context of death, or pray with another when death has touched the other personally through the loss of a family member or friend.

Over, done, finished. Death takes a life, but does not remove the memories. A lifetime of days and delights, coupled with successes, failures, sorrows, and joys, is all there to be remembered, reviewed, and recalled, but not repeated, except in memory. Photographs and letters help to get that remembering kind of talk going; so do diplomas, licenses, and the keepsakes that trigger talk of days gone by. It all adds up to virtually endless opportunities for gratitude—to God, the creator of it all; to the deceased person who might not have been thanked before, and to those who are part of the memories and may have been there with the person whose life has slipped away. Thank you, thank you, thank you.

In bereavement, many sorrowing persons need help in working through feelings of guilt at not having forgiven, not having thanked, not having appreciated, and perhaps not having been there at the end with and for another who is now out of reach and who will never come back to hear that unspoken word of love, forgiveness, apology, gratitude, affirmation. A friend can now provide that ear. A friend can encourage the bereaved to say those words that went unsaid and to express the feelings that roil within the sorrowing heart and add immeasurably to the pain of loss. And in talking to a grieving person about God in time of sorrow, a friend can open the other's hurting heart to the healing power of grace, which, of course, only God can give.

You don't have to be able to explain grace or how it works; you just have to welcome into this privileged conversation the presence of God and let the healing happen.

The other fundamental direction that the conversation can take is forward, outward, beyond immediate experience. This means talking about the afterlife.

A grief-stricken adult daughter who was awaiting her father's impending and certain death, once asked me what life would be like for him after he died. She was willing to let go of her childhood imaginings of heaven's golden streets and beautiful gardens to consider an existence with no pain and no limits on the mind's ability to comprehend ideas. She could appreciate that an existence of union with God, who is love, would mean a union of her father's heart and mind with the heart (figuratively speaking) and mind of God. "He will be able to grasp the content of all the books in the Library of Congress! Language barriers will disappear. No hatred, no enemy will ever touch him. Illness, sadness, and suffering in any form will be banished from his experience forever."

Just thinking about the "forever" dimension of her father's impending new experience of peace and happiness, and his ability now to see things from God's perspective, opened her up to a sense of awe. But what had the most calming and reassuring effect was the realization that after his death she could continue to talk to her father, that she could pray to him as well as for him, and that his help would still be available to her. She said she had the "perfect dad," their relationship had always been "great," and she found comfort in the assurance that this would continue in a new key.

But be prepared for anger to emerge in conversations about God triggered by death or, as we shall see below, disappointment. In Alice McDermott's novel *At Weddings and Wakes* (Farrar Straus Giroux, 1992), the narrator catches this nicely with references to daughter Lucy observing "the fury in Momma's movements as she walked between the bureau and the dressing table...muttering to herself all the while, slamming brushes and drawers, and in the failing darkness she would see how the anger seemed to straighten Momma's spine and set form her face....Lucy would see that, given the middle of life, loss following as it did every gain, and death and disappointment so inevitable, anger was the only appropriate emotion; that for any human being with any sense, any memory or foresight, every breath taken should be tinged with outrage" (pp. 111–12). Anger is likely to be there. It will eventually go away. It helps a lot to talk it out.

Disappointment

Any disappointment is a little death, a darkness that will eventually see some light, a defeat that is preamble to victory. Not to talk about disappointments is to delay the arrival of both light and victory. But you can't talk about your disappointments unless someone offers you a sympathetic ear. Even more important is for someone with a sympathetic eye to notice your hidden disappointments and to literally see through any protective front you may have raised. Once exposed, either through disclosure or discovery, a disappointment can be a talking point for conversation about God. "Where is (or was) God in all of this?" is a central question in the conversation that follows upon a genuine disappointment.

Knowing what it is like to bear up under the weight of disappointment is excellent preparation to encourage a person to play the helpful role of a sympathetic ear. When you were down, how would you have reacted if someone asked, "Would you like to talk about it?" "Tell me about it; how did it all happen?" "When and where did things begin to unravel?" "I know you had your heart set on it, but let's start looking ahead now at other possibilities."

Perhaps another formulation of words would have been preferable to your own ear. Think now what those words might have been. Consider how you might direct similar words to a disappointed friend as openers for talk that begins with a downside experience, but can lead to an upside awareness of the hand of God reaching out through disappointment to touch the person in need of help.

There is an options game to be played in the wake of any disappointment. It is not helpful to begin that game by looking backward and asking what should I not have done, or what might I have done differently. What's done is done and there is usually no point in beating yourself over the head with options not taken or the memory of bad moves made. Looking forward, however, is an altogether different story. Let's see now, what have we learned? That one didn't work. That was not a wise choice. Timing was not good in that case. No need to look back; let's look ahead. What are the best options for our next move? Let's see.

C. S. Lewis has his "senior devil" Screwtape instruct the "junior devil" Wormwood to use disappointment, a universal human experience, as a weapon in tempting the unsuspecting, tricking them into believing that God has somehow injured them, unfairly depriving them of something to which they have a right. "The Enemy [i.e., God] allows this disappointment to occur on the threshold of every human endeavor. It occurs when the boy who has been enchanted in the nursery by *Stories from the Odyssey* buckles down to really learning Greek. It occurs when lovers have got married and begin the real task of learning to live together. In every department of life it marks the transition from dreaming aspiration to laborious doing" (*The Screwtape Letters*, Letter II, para. 3). Screwtape goes on to explain that God "takes this risk" of permitting disappointment because he wants human beings to be free. "Desiring their freedom, He therefore refuses to carry them, by their mere affections and habits, to any of the goals which He sets before them: He leaves them to 'do it on their own.' And there lies our opportunity. But also, remember, there lies our danger. If once they get through this initial dryness successfully, they become much less dependent on emotion and therefore much harder to tempt" *(Ibid.)*. Hence the importance of talking it out and avoiding mistaking the presence of disappointment for the absence of God.

Lost Opportunity

Opportunities that are lost haunt the memory of just about everyone. For most, that thought is reduced to manageable size by the reassuring memory of opportunities that were indeed taken and brought with them the experience of achievement, success, and satisfaction. That state of mind is a congenial setting for a word of thanks to God whose providence put the opportunity within reach. (Not to thank God for facilitating your good fortune is still another lost opportunity!)

Lost opportunities, the kind that have you kicking yourself around the block, have a way of flattening hope and deflating self-esteem. To make the situation worse, realization that an opportunity is no longer at hand but lost forever, is cause for some to conclude that the hand of a punishing God pulled that opportunity out from under them, like a rug snatched from underfoot. God doesn't operate that way. If you are not convinced of that, you should be talking to someone about God in the circumstance of lost opportunity. If, on the other hand, you can see God's guiding hand moving in the fashion of an orchestra conductor who coaxes the best from all willing players who use their talents freely and wisely, you can facilitate, in the context of opportunities seized or lost, a great conversation about God's providence and the uses of human freedom.

In any lost opportunity there is a slight echo of death, of that unrepeatable onceness that characterizes life. That familiar, often haunting, awareness of the irreversibility of time that has passed can coil itself around a human heart and wring out hope when indecision or wrong decision is responsible for an opportunity lost. What do you talk about when this is the case?

First, you talk about God who gives you freedom to choose, but refuses to make your choices for you. Quite a compliment to you, but a burden as well for you to have to carry through life. That line of conversation takes you into the mysterious relationship between divine power and divine omniscience, on the one hand, and human freedom on the other. Why doesn't God force us to do what is best for us? How can we humans veto God's positive will for us and just go ahead and do something that an all-wise God knows to be bad for us?

Second, and much more practically speaking, you talk to yourself and friends about how you can recover your lost opportunity, not by rewinding the reel and having another shot at a decision already taken, but by providing a new opportunity for someone else. Using your resourcefulness to create a fresh opportunity for someone other than yourself helps, by definition, to get you out of yourself. It has a marvelously therapeutic quality to it. You become absorbed in "making up" for the opportunity you lost by creating a good opportunity for someone else. Whether or not that person takes this new opportunity is not your worry; it is just a part of life with which you are already quite familiar.

There is plenty of room in all this for prayer. Pray that good ideas will come to you. Pray that the resources will fall into place that make it possible to translate the idea into a challenging project or program. Pray for the success of the project and, of course, offer a prayer of thanks to the Lord of all opportunity, to the God whose providence builds bridges over failures and puts hope in the heart of anyone striving to be fully human. As an ancient saying puts it so well, "The glory of God is the human person fully alive." Opportunities produce life for both those who provide them as well as those who take them.

40. To Anyone Who Asks

Think of those times when someone may have asked you about God. Children ask such questions readily. From adults, questions about God arise in all sorts of settings. Predictably, they will arise in hospitals and funeral homes. Unpredictably, they will crop up, as we've seen, in the family and among friends. But they will also become part of the conversation with virtual strangers on airplanes and trains, buses and taxicabs, and with acquaintances over lunch, or workplace associates at the water cooler.

In religious settings, of course, someone may very well ask you for your thoughts about God and the things of God. That is to be expected. But what happens all too rarely in religious settings is the creation of an environment for non-ritualized conversation, for free exchange of ideas and spontaneous faith-sharing. More often than not, in my experience, it will be laypersons, not clergy, who organize prayer groups and invite members of the congregation to come together informally, off schedule, in the presence of God to discuss the things of God. By off schedule, I mean that the gathering is unrelated to the normal schedule of religious services and can often occur in private homes rather than chapels or other places dedicated to prayer.

It can be a rich experience to invite a pastor, rabbi, or other member of the clergy to sit in on these home meetings and respond to the questions: Who is God for you? How do you approach God in prayer? How do you imagine or visualize the God to whom you pray?

You will get questions about God and the efficacy of prayer sometimes in letters that you are expected to answer. Some of these questions arise not infrequently on the editorial page or in news stories that you respond to only in your mind. Forming your response is in fact a form of prayer. It can engage you in a personal reenactment of Jacob wrestling with the angel. Nothing wrong with spiritual struggles; why not talk about them with other persons of faith? Why not draw upon your own experience to answer the questions of others, however and whenever they come to you?

This "To Anyone Who Asks" category would, of course, include those you might meet in an Internet chat room. The anonymity of the Internet is likely to encourage probing questions; your anonymous answers can permit self-disclosure without self-identification, a consideration of capital importance whenever you venture into cyberspace.

Two post-middle-age adults, one male and the other female, who know each other through a mutual friend but have not yet met in person, correspond by means of e-mail. The gentleman in this exchange is an acquaintance of mine. He has experienced recently a religious conversion, serious illness, and business reversals from which he is recovering nicely. His e-mail correspondent picked up on this with a direct question: "Do you suppose that all the things that have happened to you in the last couple of years seem to be leading to a sea-change in your life?" She then recounts the events—renewed interest in religion, new friends, experience of "trust in God's loving presence," and goes on to ask: "Has this readied, strengthened, and prepared you for what apparently was the next event: cancer?"

She then tells him that he's been "given the gift of a couple of scary health problems, one or the other of which typically leads to a deep reflection on mortality, on how you've been spending your time, treasure, talents, and how you want to change the rest of your life, should you be so lucky as to have said life. With the gift of your newly found faith and supportive community, you got through all the hard stuff. Looks as if you were given a second chance. Did this perhaps ready you for the next event, your client skipping out?"

She continues: "Your biggest and best client leaves you with zip except bills. Does this seem to be a timely coincidence? After all these years, why lose Big Client now? What in the world is happening? Why now? This isn't a failure that could be attributed to you. It's the failure of an S.O.B. deadbeat to pay bills." And then, she notes, "Through some quirky and marvelous turn of events, we are introduced to one another—not as strangers, but as two people whose lives have almost intersected at several points. And now you're wondering, What now?" Her e-mail reflection moves on to talk about God. "The reason it's somewhat easy for me to identify just Who is at work here, is that your story is also my story." And she goes on to recount her story of an automobile accident, memory loss, recovery, turning to prayer, finding satisfaction in rendering pastoral care to the sick and homebound, realizing the need for training and taking it to qualify for employment in a new career of service that requires her "to show up and listen." She ends the message by leaving him with a prayer composed by St. Francis de Sales: "Do not look forward to what might happen tomorrow; the same everlasting Father who cares for you today will take care of you tomorrow and every day. Either he will shield you from suffering, or he will give you unfailing strength to bear it. Be at peace, then, and put aside all anxious thoughts and imaginations."

Needless to say, that conversation about God is to be continued.

41. To Anyone Who Is Waiting to Hear

I knew a prominent and popular public figure who spent the last year of his life in a hospital bed gravely ill. His wife, a woman of deep faith, sat quietly by his side through each long day, well into the night. They spoke, of course, at intervals throughout the day and evening, but the longer intervals, much longer, were filled with silence. I would see her there, on my occasional visits, as an anchor of hope. Her peaceful presence filled the room with reassurance and calm. She would read a bit, pray, and occasionally write notes and letters to well-wishers who offered their prayers and support from afar. In one such note to me, she mentioned that she too was praying, just in case "Anyone might be listening." She was one of those you will often find who are "waiting to hear" an answer to prayer.

The wait is a test not only of patience, but also of faith. If faith is the act by which you entrust yourself to God, the absence of an answer constitutes a greater demand on your faith and calls for an even larger deposit of trust. All you can do is trust, and wait. And no one who has been through it will ever suggest that it is easy.

What can you say about God to someone who is waiting to hear? You know that he or she is waiting to hear from God, not you, but your voice can, in the tradition of the prophets, be a conduit for the voice of God. Don't even attempt it if you have no experience of God in prayer. Don't try if you are not yourself, however clumsily and awkwardly, in touch by faith with God. If you are, however, in touch as best you can be, then give it a try. You live by faith, not by sight; so don't think that you have to "see" God and literally "hear" God's voice in order to be able to offer your voice as a channel for God's wisdom to reach those who are "waiting to hear."

More often than not, serious illness will prompt the prayer and a deep desire for a cure will frame the hoped-for response. Ever so gently, a human voice like yours can point out that the eventual, and at some point in every life, the inevitable response to the request for a cure is, "No, there will be no cure now for you, but something better that is beyond all imagining awaits you now with God for all eternity." Let the talk turn to the eternity of God, the changelessness of God, the fidelity of God, the joy that God takes now in the presence of countless humans who, since the origins of the human race, have gone home to heaven from deathbeds, battlefields, and death-dealing accidents and illnesses of every kind. Let the talk turn to the ill person's friends who are now present to

God in heaven, but who used to be close to the person who is "waiting to hear" when they were here on earth—in the home, in the circle of family and friends. "They too have passed through death to life," you can tell your friend; "they too are praying and waiting for you."

42. Praying Together

"Can we pray together?" is a question heard more frequently now, I believe, than was the case in years gone by. At least, it seems so to me.

The organizers of a group of young working adults who meet about once a month in a Washington bar under the rubric of "Theology on Tap," asked me that question recently just before I was about to address the group, 150 strong, gathered on a Tuesday evening in front of a band stand and next to the second floor bar at Lulu's, a downtown tavern that provides them with space and microphone at no charge, grateful to have a pay-for-drink crowd on what would otherwise be an off night for the business.

They are a serious, faith-committed group of young career professionals who use these get-togethers for networking, friend making, and faith sharing around theological topics arranged in "six-packs," sets of six presentations in the fall and the spring, by speakers with appropriate credentials and name recognition. The Cardinal Archbishop of Washington appeared on the program twice drawing about 300 hearers each time! (And this, by the way, not without some criticism from older Catholics who get their exercise by lifting their eyebrows. They were "shocked," they said, to think that their spiritual leader would meet with young people in a bar. The Cardinal responded to the criticism by reaffirming his availability to meet with young people anywhere they liked, if it provided the opportunity for him to dialogue with them about faith and theology.)

In any case, we did pray, or I should say, they prayed for me as we huddled, five or six of us, off to the side, before I went up on the platform to talk about workplace spirituality under the heading of "Work: More Than a Paycheck." At the conclusion of the talk, the lead organizer of the group ended the meeting with a closing prayer. Both prayers, at the opening and close of this session, were led by laypersons, spoken in their own words, from the heart, on the topic of the evening, and to a God in whom they had great confidence. Why has it taken so long for us to grow comfortable praying aloud in the presence of others?

Praying together is an exercise for two, or four, or many more, depending on the circumstances. Recall that earlier in this part (in the section under the heading of "Spouse") I outlined a praying-together scenario where spouses or a larger "circle of friends" could literally gather in a circle around a selection from Scripture or some other appropriate text, read it aloud, and simply permit it to occasion privileged moments of faith-sharing. Spoken reflections, prompted by the text, allow the Spirit to speak to the group. In these settings the presence of God is palpable as the word of God comes alive in the hearts of those who dare to pray together.

43. Goodbye, Farewell

They call it a "prayer of commendation," the closing prayer said as mourners prepare to leave the church at the end of a funeral and move out to the cemetery for a final farewell. "Goodbye" is never final when the spoken word marks a departure through death. You continue to converse in prayer with dear ones who have gone home to God, and with God about those you have commended to his care in a ritual farewell. God is indeed with the departed, and the departed person is now with God in keeping with your expressed hope when you said, "God be with ye." Goodbye.

Farewell means just that—may you fare well now in your new life. Faith enables those who say, "Goodbye, farewell," to become convinced that the battle is indeed over, the victory has been won, and the person no longer physically present to you is now completely present to God.

"Goodbye, farewell, so long forever..." are just words from a song. "Forever" simply does not fit the reality of separation from those you've known and loved in this world. Not only will you be reunited with them in eternal life, you can and should pray to them while your journey continues in this life. They have newly acquired powers of intercession, and through their intercession you will receive what is beyond your human power to obtain for yourself on earth. Believe it. You can count on it!

Take a moment or two in your own personal prayer to reverse the direction of those two words. Say goodbye and farewell to yourself. May God be with me. May I fare well this day and every day. What does it mean for God to be "with" me? What is required of me by way of cooperation if I am to "fare well" as God's plan for me would have me fare?

You've often thought of carfare, bus fare, train fare, air-fare. The fare is your wherewithal for passage, for forward motion, for progress. May I fare well, Lord, in every stage of my journey, in every step I take.

Those to whom you have said, "Goodbye, farewell," in ritual closure to your life together on earth, are well positioned to assist you in maintaining your determination to "be with God," and to fare as well as possible in your journey now without them at your side. They are there, really, but you just can't see them. You can find them in your prayer.

Afterword

This book is a sequel to *A Book of Quiet Prayer* (Paulist Press, 2006). To formalize the link between the two, I repeat, by way of "afterword," a reflection of St. Augustine on "Prayer and Desire" taken from his Letter to Proba.

His thoughts will, I hope, help you to continue to think about enlarging both the desire for God in prayer and the capacity to receive from God the good things that are held in store by God for those who ask for them in prayer. These are words to be read slowly and aloud—to yourself in a quiet setting, to others in a faith-sharing environment. Don't rush. Just listen to Augustine.

Why in our fear of not praying as we should, do we turn to so many things, to find what we should pray for? Why do we not say instead, in the words of the psalmist: "I have asked one thing from the Lord, this is what I will seek: to dwell in the Lord's house all the days of my life, to see the graciousness of the Lord, and to visit his temple." There, the days do not come and go in succession, and the beginning of one day does not mean the end of another; all days are one, simultaneously and without end, and the life lived out in these days has itself no end.

So that we might obtain this life of happiness, he who is true life itself taught us to pray, not in many words as though speaking longer could gain us a hearing. After all, we pray to one who, as the Lord himself tells us, knows what we need before we ask for it.

Why he should ask us to pray, when he knows what we need before we ask him, may perplex us if we do not realize that our Lord and God does not want to know what we want (for he cannot fail to know it) but wants us rather to exercise our desire through our prayers, so that we might be able to receive what he is preparing to give us. His gift is very great indeed, but our capacity is too small and limited to receive it. That is why we are told "Enlarge your desires, do not bear the yoke with unbelievers."

The deeper our faith, the stronger our hope, the greater our desire, the larger will be our capacity to receive that gift, which is very great indeed. "No eye has seen it"; it has no color. "No ear has heard it"; it has no sound. "It has not entered man's heart"; man's heart must enter into it.

In this faith, hope, and love, we pray always with unwearied desire. However, at set times and seasons we also pray to God in words, so that by these signs we may instruct ourselves and mark the progress we have made in our desire, and spur ourselves on to deepen it. The more fervent the desire, the more worthy will be its fruit. When the Apostle [Paul] tells us: "Pray without ceasing," he means this: Desire unceasingly that life of happiness which is nothing if not eternal, and ask it of him who alone is able to give it.

Also by William J. Byron, SJ

Quadrangle Considerations (1989)

Finding Work without Losing Heart (1995)

Take Courage: Psalms of Support and Encouragement
(editor, 1995)

Answers from Within (1998)

Jesuit Saturdays (2000)

A Book of Quiet Prayer (2006)*

Individuarian Observations (2007)

Words at the Wedding (2007)*

*available from Paulist Press